Spirit of a Dove

Spirit of a Dove

Jaco Jonathan Maritz

WestBow
PRESS
A DIVISION OF THOMAS NELSON

WestBow Press books may be ordered through booksellers or by contacting:

WestBow Press
A Division of Thomas Nelson
1663 Liberty Drive
Bloomington, IN 47403
www.westbowpress.com
1-(866) 928-1240

Because of the dynamic nature of the Internet, any web addresses or
links contained in this book may have changed since publication and
may no longer be valid. The views expressed in this work are solely those
of the author and do not necessarily reflect the views of the publisher,
and the publisher hereby disclaims any responsibility for them.

Certain stock imagery © Thinkstock.
Any people depicted in stock imagery provided by Thinkstock are
models, and such images are being used for illustrative purposes only.

ISBN: 978-1-4497-5718-2 (e)
ISBN: 978-1-4497-5719-9 (sc)

Library of Congress Control Number: 2012911162

Printed in the United States of America

WestBow Press rev. date: 6/21/2012

Preface

—— ⊰ ❋ ⊱ ——

I had long wondered about the need for an introductory note. At last I concluded, on the advice of my contending conscience, to write something down as it relates to the transliteration of Scripture. Art for art's sake, as the saying goes, can perhaps take more liberties than it ought and has been laid too often for the sake of justification at the annoying corners of transgression. Liberty allows for art, but art does not allow for liberty. This is especially true in respect to art that wishes to reflect on a sacred subject. Nonetheless, if the aspiring artist trembles too much in fear of sacrilege, it makes me consider a neurotic guilt over integrity as the cause of his or her apparent rectitude. Let us take an obvious example: Milton's *Paradise Lost*, an epic poem that masterfully embellishes the fall of man. Surely even the keenest contemporary critic would lower the voice of their grumbling in light of Milton's evident art and transparent sincerity.

My narrative or representation of Scripture can be, with a superficial glance, considered as an abbreviation of the Old and New Testaments. I should rather call it a sample—or better yet, an extract—as a true abbreviation would have been entirely different in its scope and content. As such, the stories from the Bible were transcribed without a determined focus on the actual line-by-line detail, and they fall, therefore, below the order of consistent historical fact, having been subjected and augmented to the preference of an easy and fetching read. In spite of this principle, I was invariably conscious throughout the process to uphold the spirit of the Scripture, being always ready to dismiss a too-pleasurable approximation which might have disfavored the duty to truth.

The arbitrary and extracting approach I took made the narrative easily obedient to the passion of the characters or events—this instead of the intrinsic theology that is naturally yielded when the actual Scripture is read outright. If there were a swaying apprehension to dodge theology, it was for the sake of the brevity of the text. Still, theology itself need not be the aversive or ossified concept that it has been made out to be; in fact, the partial intent of my narrative is to place a few theological concepts into view and on an equal and interesting footing with the animated stories.

As far as the style, it is perhaps best not to say too much; yet I will add some background here for the sake of curiosity. I was determined to avoid the missteps of a too-eager apprentice and kept at hand the advice of Coleridge. In his *Biographia Literaria*, he tells how he had "pruned ... to tame the swell and glitter both of thought and diction ..." He went on to explain how the "parasite plants of youthful poetry had insinuated themselves ..." On my part, I had edited the narrative in this wisdom, though not consistently with the same zeal, and had clipped or uprooted many an odd or pretentious rose from a bed of common flowers. An occasional metaphor or delightful poetic form had insisted or asserted itself too strongly against my editing hand, and I had relented to prune in the belief that the proud, outstanding flower is not necessarily an imputation against the common order of daisies or a humble bristle bush.

Chapter 1

───────────── ⊰ ❈ ⊱ ─────────────

This is a small account of history, composed by means of glancing and breezing through the holy Scriptures and scooping up the precipitate that insensibly collected and stood out along the way. The habit of Scripture is detail, and this habit thinks nothing of adding page after page, of bravely working toward something far off in the distance. Without the same patience and endurance, the version at hand makes a short and prejudicial flight, like a listless butterfly in no mood for greens. And since there is ambition for the ornate, on the slight encouragement of imagination, heaven will be acknowledged first, along with its gardens and the days before mankind.

Heaven was placed advantaged, its members full of light; it was as though they circled round and round the Source of light, as stars in flight or cosmic orbs in pleasant swings, and they had their songs, if flight could sing—sing of unending dawn.

The Architect must have laid this place on a pleasant spot or raised it up on an angle or a slope, because it always caught, between the day and night, the morning light. With this perpetual and familiar heat, feasts hung from unnumbered trees, and flowers, not inferior in color, dressed the rivers and the lakes. The shrubs and ferns thrived here as well, their fruit shaped different from the standard organ of a tree. In its place, they gave happy, fleshy green and had a seeming joy and exclamation in the shape of spreading meadows that, slow-moving, moved toward a central light. Though the gardens of heaven were generally lush, there was no wish toward a jungle; therefore, here and there were passing trails that coiled around and, by some unknown means (and yet apparent, innate strength), invited nearby angels to indulge and join their gliding motion to the throne of God.

All heaven's paths were glad, and some were even sportive, as they served within their turns to help one marvel at the first-created things—originals that would serve as templates for the pending paradise. There a flock of little birds, their flight from tree to tree, mad as with the workings of joy, and their loud song, not careless but loud in the workings of praise. And here lambs and lions intermixed, serene among the orders of a multitude of primordial beasts: some satiated, lying around in easy rest, some grazing, but grazing, filled, as in delight.

Over there stood an angel in his park, tending to this stretch of garden. There was such a duty in his charge that he did not deign to casually look around. The angel had such pose, such godlike state, such single-minded circumspection, that one ought better hurry on, taking no privilege or liberty that proximity might allow.

Without full knowledge of this time, one must use different means to bring history to the front, and imagination is useful, even when its fidelity is questioned. When one moves about on uncertain and speculative ground, it is best to move on; haste helps the peering mind from getting into too much trouble. Onward, then, is best, and onward to more great beings, who, by degrees of state and glory, lived and moved about in this superlative place. These seemed weightless, being spirit, and pure—of light wherein no darkness or even shade could hide; yet they were full of gravity and power, the style and work of glory. They had attractive orders, too many to describe: angels, seraphim, cherubim, and others unpronounced.

There were sounds all around, some different and some the same, none suppressed and none meant to surpass; a hum within the adhesive air, within the trees and water springs, within the hills and, higher up and even from afar, the Orion and the Pleiades, a gentle music of some cosmic pulse. In this way blew heaven her good sounds, a first fruit of herself that needed to come out with irrepressible exhalation. She, heaven, poured only from her overflow, her soft, familiar, and continuous song in which there was no outside composition, no added glitter, no need to sift the sound. One could even imagine their cadence or their shapes (if sound had shape) and view their little forms pick up from lush verdure or starry constellation, perhaps as playful strings or fluid ribbons passing through the air and racing, easy, to the throne.

Another current was in this place and, from the throne, lent itself to the striking doctrines of glory—a theology of movement, as it were, a perspective of the revolutions of all things around God. Its substance was blissful light that—all around its course, radiant and outward—all sorts of colors decked. Some lights were dispensed in showy streaks, high, leaping toward a blushing sky. Others were fastidious and would unto a flower cling. In this way, the hues cheered heaven on, eager colors that refused, by all the life around, to merely lie around benign or shine with small benevolence. Their shine divided from the rainbow round the throne and thereby reflected in some degree a part of God. He was the light's agency and its proposing voice. But the most sweet light and mesmeric color was in Him, who glowed as seven suns at noon, as a splendid flame of blazing white.

At this juncture, time had not yet moved to exhibit paradise or mankind. These had not yet been created, and man had not yet been formed. His blueprint was still inside his God. Still, even so, of mankind's future fate there lay a confessing glimpse in God, whose very corporeal side, within the glory clouds, revealed a secret and astonishing wound! It looked as though God's side had been struck with a perplexing force—that God even had in parts of Him some flesh. And when one ought only to admire His glory, one is too interested, when peering back into the past, in the insistence of the once-wounded God; and one is baffled and cannot instructively put to words how it can be—only that one knows He was and is and is to be, and is all of this at once. It seems there will later be a dispute, something inflexible that will rise up, yet it is too far future for one to see Him slain and raised.

Now there was another being during this early time who also could not see. The wound eluded him. At first he was amazing, that great and flourishing angel around the throne. How he walked high and easy and shone like a sun. There he pitched above the throne; there he lifted his spear against God and sang his most irregular song, he who had the best song and the preeminent, composing tone now striving for some awful, higher note, and playing with words of self-exultation.

This angel gave out an indecent verse with self-assuming application, a lyric borne within himself that grew with rapid, thirsty growth. This angel sang of himself, not God. In this way began Lucifer to be adverse; he was the first of the angels to be shaped into a devil and the first who broke the bounds of dateless peace, seizing violence for a violent sake, as he bent his spear toward his Lord. But this affront and this arming of himself did not rival the arm of God, which quickly doomed the audacious strike with a guarding strike from Michael's sword.

Throughout the vastness of this realm, all the angels halted in their stance. They were concerned by this new sound they heard— the sudden clamor of a weapon's clash. It was perplexing, because it had in it the meaning of dispute. The awful sound survived, and the trouble rolled across the planes of heaven. It unfolded slowly like a warbling murmur and then rose upward, drawing up sounds of increasing dissonance: the discord made between a sword and spear, the flapping of angels' wings, inharmonious in this scene as each archangel tried to rise above the other in the sparkling air.

Michael was more content and swift and had himself reared up as though to slay. Lucifer, his foe beneath, thrust terribly to spoil the advantage of the one above.

Now Lucifer, called Satan from here on, had begun to fret of his mutinous plan. The incessant grip of Michael had converted his proud hope to something of mortification, and so, as though to gain by deceit what he could not otherwise obtain by strength, he called to the lower angels for some help. He called out through subtleties and, through his beauty, called in charm.

Satan was crowned chief deceiver. This was not for nothing, as he was the first to deceive his own peers. He deserved that bad crown, because he deceived, through his charm and the gravity of his size, a third of the bewildered angels. This third, who had just before walked with regal poise, now began to bend inside toward an iniquitous deviance; it was not that their splendid forms at once became opaque—they were not immediately vulnerable—but rather, a slow infection began to snuff out their vital force. Perhaps it was like the worm to the flower or a parasite that does not wish to betray itself; it advocates for tolerance. Nonetheless, these unfortunate angels had their willing crime—and thus their fate—in dying; but it was not death as death is understood in flesh, in those who have their bodies made of earth. Rather, it was a kind of death where dying is perpetual, an immortality that always feels the approach of a miserable end, yet never reaches it, being always excluded from the life of God.

Then for a moment this self-appointed chief appeared more daring—having grown with a cutthroat grab his very own host—and more proud, with a lifted head and wings like a serpentine dragon, which had from his grove awoken. His dragon-form was apt; it obeyed the requisite demands of his strength, the request of blasphemy, the excuse to be cruel, and the intent for usurpation. Yet more bold than this shape was a voice that arrived like thunder in a gust: God's voice, which called out to Michael and asked him of the tidings.

Now this good angel answered God and said, "Oh, Maker, all good, some horror has risen from my feet. It is the same one whom I'd struck off from his zenith. It is this prior Lucifer, who now in a strong attempt around my legs dares to coil. And what else he does is awful: He has learned his new darkness well and weaves it to make his own form misshape. He lengthens out with scaly tail and seems to be leviathan. That's not all, there is more horror here: he has seized a throng of angels, those who had stood nearby his snatching tail. These have been translated to evil and are now eager with this same one's zeal."

Again the voice within the gust, and God replied, "Daylong, now you have been fighting your peer and have been slow in driving him with your sword, which is as a yoke upon a wild ox, and have led this odd angel from his pleasant plot crosswise to the outer edge. Now make an end of this—my strength fits you—and toss Satan from the starry cliff as though you are a champion, as though you throw a lightning disc."

God spoke, and the foe was flung, and as Satan flew downward (his speed and way were instructive) he did not repent of his loss. As he fell, he construed another plan in mid-flight, only now it was for wrath, no longer for mere usurpation. The fall, his muse, sang for him of potent hate. And in hate and partner-seeking, he stretched up his tail, his sting, which struck to catch a third of once bright stars.

These fallen dropped out of heaven, though not yet to their future hell; they dropped down to a lower sphere, a plane, a second heaven of some sort that hovered high above the planes of earth.

Chapter 2

—⋄❈⋄—

The second realm of heaven had at first no prejudice of style; it had an incumbent neutrality and was a place yet to be managed. Its plasticity was susceptible to the darkness of the newcomers, and their light, a kind of moonless gleam of night, lit up the vastness of the ruinscape. Here they fell and stood, all lost. Their guide and captor, Satan, was so misplaced that he took time to reassure himself. He drifted mute toward a rocky spot and felt himself undone.

Here one might find pity convenient and useful as one tries with effort to make sense of this scene. But it is forbidden to grant to those dark spirits what might incline to mercy. It is by prudent choice that one does not aim to tame a brood of adders. Some other law applies to them, a judgment that at once obeys all love and all justice even as it forms these fallen angels' imputation and their just reproach.

And so demons, as they existed then and exist now, are all lost and all cruel, because they are not souls but spirit entities that live as by a single element. They are sequestered in their innate shapes and confined as by a single quality, so that when their state is turned, it cannot be turned again.

A soul is different. It has wide shores, in a figurative sense: a land along the sea that lets its soil be dipped by waters of all sorts; it swallows some sea and takes the currents as a guide.

A soul has soil. It can be a host and can produce another through birth. If the land of the soul grows near a storm or night, it will reform and shape itself in some way: perhaps a spiky rock that to the night winds leans; or if the land might be a grassy fold—its nurture from morning mists and dew, not storms—there will grow here and there a happy little tuft. The soul in a sense is a living house that can, unlike spirits, be born again in death.

Now the fallen host stood around, aghast yet mute, their notes in whispers only and in sighs; but later on, as the demons spread across the place, their moans became distinct. The faded sounds of groaning from a nearby cliff came from a spirit who sat there in gargoyle form; it moaned upon the cold, black rock. Other sounds too through the air began to tumble and seemed to lonely drop, and drop as if too loaded for the crampy air. In this place, even sound was not free; it would slowly lift and drop, perhaps as corpulent dragons in their massive flight.

Some distance farther off was the sound of heavy breath. It was a brood of dragons that had taken off in flight—these had once been angels of a higher rank—and the forms of feathered wings were exchanged, from spite, for scales of plumeless drakes. They had left the larger throng of fallen ones and had by slow and circling swoops around their peers this plane begun to try. They had seen a distant sulfur flame and taken it for a wishful hope, and flew there in spite of all the gravity, with dauntless strokes of wings and might. Their act or flight around the place was not for curiosity; no, their minds were nearer to ambition and their thoughts were to hurry and find or usurp the best grounds here that might be found.

This realm or second heaven was meant in time to emulate the third in its design and was not formed as if it had the business of a hell. It had no deliberate profanity and was largely empty. It sang the song of barrenness but sang its song in hope. God had made this second plane and had stretched it out so far that it had made its way to earth. It was rolled out into the cosmic space as the moon is seen to roll, to have its blush at night; and its honor and bloom were to be subservient.

Yet the fallen first took hold of this place before human spirits took it for their private gardens, and in the instant of the demons' downward plunge, this place began to cleave, perhaps by their tainted presence or by their pestilent art. When they ought rather to have lived in and confined themselves to moroseness, which was nearest to repentance for their state, they moved their thoughts and deeds to the level of spite and the energy of fear.

Their dead hearts took the assailable place and hurt it everywhere. A little fountain that before had trickled with a whimpering stream was now urged to borrow fire and strange smell and to misuse itself, spewing lava from its pore. Elsewhere too, the same trouble coerced the land: chaos became tenable and order was in doubt. It was all madness as the throng scurried across the plane—some in groups and some alone, some frightened and mindless, some in rage and with superior strength and demon rank, oppressing their own peers. A long-lasting night had descended, and with it anarchy, false freedom. In time each demon found its spot. Most gathered in clunky groups, sundry tribes and factions, each after their antecedent angelic type, with fear already making its divide.

There in a large, flat field, the grass knee-long and wilted white as under strain of winter, a thousand kindred spirits grouped and roamed. These had changed their forms to that of bears or bear-like beasts. Their temper was poisoned and their delight was rage; these were violent spirits and contagious, because they stirred each other up. Their violence at first came in that bad licensor of soft abuse—in wit and awful humor, in satire or sarcasm, in cold words warmly dressed—but for these spirits, words could not hold their vicious stamp. They tied their tongues, and on their beastly paws they lashed out at each other with wild blows, with groans and swipes, the variety of a bear gone mad.

There was another place nearby—a gap inside a cliff—and inside its cave grew ruin. It would have been better for the cave had the walls been burdened by a brood of bats retired upside down, rather than the abominable creatures that had descended even further than their mates. These upside-down creatures in the cave had a far more revolting suggestion to their forms; they made themselves most spitefully adverse, a direct invective against the stately and dignified designs of the art of God.

These, being spirits, could naturally alter their misshapen outer veil to whatever was the form of their inner purpose. To know what drove them to this abominable end, one must know their start, their previous form on the side of light. This brood had once been seraphim, and they carried, as though from their original shape, some symmetry or equal shape, as it were—only now it was for darkness and for opposition. They passed as harpies, a Lilith species, grim birds, self-smitten by sinewy connections: a lone, long neck for a grinning woman's head, her teeth athirst, and the body of a bird with feathers worn and spare. In this form they spread through the cave, shuffling about below the steeps and moaning vain.

The great fiend—Lucifer, the fallen one—had stood murmuring in loss through all this time. Then he woke as by hate, not pain, and saw himself enthroned again—his dream before and now yet again—enthroned as God superior. Yet a lesser throne was fated for him, a lesser kingdom for a lesser king. Here again his prideful will began; he would create his kingdom on this lower plane, uplift himself in any way he wished, and have his gang invent against God. For this reason, Satan began to spy around. He found a few lower spirits, those who were by weakness condemned to be subservient. For them he had some words—sweet, nursing words—and sent them to high and hollow places where the scattered might be found, to call them back as a collection. These went out to all the corners of their realm and returned in time with all the demon-host, who grouped and stood compounded on a flat plane. In their sorts they stood—in concord by the sum of sight but in discord by a closer and more daring sight.

Pomp was here invented, its first stage found by Satan, who took it for his use. He stood on a rocky cliff above them all, proud and large, thereby to cure his absent glory. Beneath him, and first along the myriad rim, some bulkier spirits stayed; they had taken their line ambitiously, and a scuffle had made it sure. What was begun by the stronger was followed in the same way by the weaker; each would the other repulse, by threat or force, to get a nearer place up front, to force the smaller demons outward. After each had found his spot and rendered himself important, they all set their eyes on Satan.

But these eyes were not supplicant, were not made for worship. They knew the false throne that he had taken, and in their fears they wondered how this throne would reign. Satan did not have skill enough in charm to run this far-out crew, but charm was not needed when his arms had might enough. He began his address.

"Friends, I have no lifelong regret for what has happened; such a mood is too late for us at any rate. Our blow is complete, and our Smiter is strong. Instead of the spoil that would above us temptingly hover, we'll have this lower place for us to plunder. Here too is desire, and if our former heaven can be seen no more, we'll view it here and make it sure and beautiful. If we spend a little of ourselves (are we not like Him, divine?), we can lay another foundation, make a mark for ourselves, and have our own style as we like. There are no flowers here that could waste our cares, nor false demeanor that should make us bow continually to Him, nor a forced prescription for a worship song.

"No, from now on, appoint your own songs, and in them do not neglect your self-respect. You're stars still, and soon you will have a better color and a shine. I say, let goodness takes its boring place; it pleases me to yawn. Why take the plighted course of good? I think it's better for some bad to be in good. Let's take this other vector: I'll be commended as its prince; I'll be respected by you all; I'll steer our new progression.

"You know well that a sense of order should apply here, especially while we seem suppressed, while we learn this thing called darkness. I will try this other policy, my invented paradigm: the way of fear, not love. I discern in it a better working order, a better way to order things around.

"Then there's that other point, a rumor of a hell. It's said that we'll all land there. It's printed within God—some words He spoke upon our fall (I heard Him when I tumbled down) of a keen place He had kept for us and a keen desire to hurl us there upon a far-off day. Perhaps we can outwit His plans, for as yet I think we're not completely hopeless and lost. See, here we stand, still close beneath the curtain of the higher realm, near the deep above, where, scattered here and there are gateways to the throne. My plan is to go and hover near a portal, to prompt it for access and so invite myself through it.

"Heaven thinks of me as *outcast*, a title I find small because I think I shall be *thief*. Toward heaven I'll then steal, upward glide within the spiral gate, and pass behind the upward-looking guards. I won't blame for them my clandestine pass: the fault is in the makeup of the place: the praise too loud, the air too bright. It's their defense for my escape. Within a rosebush I'll hide, and if it can't hold me, I'll move bower to bower, as a restless bird might hop from sweet flower to sweet fruit. It is my sweetness to cheat my way toward the Smiter's throne, and once there to play the part of a loiterer, to overhear domestic secrets of the house of God and to learn of this future hell. In this way I can provide you with intelligence

"Meanwhile, you, here, make some divination. Labor to plunder this lower place. I sense it only seems this lean, giving us falsely its hard face. Perhaps the land itself is by us repulsed. It's no matter, we'll take it for a slave and make the most of slavery. Build me a palace in the deep, and for yourselves construct lesser structures as you desire. Now, let it be done. I'm on my way."

Chapter 3

——— ❧ ✖ ❧ ———

God completed all the future in the past, inasmuch as He, being eternal, holds the future for the past. Yet He, infinite and almighty, had by His skill set the future independently. On this point He had started off with self-consultation—the lovely Being with Himself in a subtle conversation of thoughts by three-yet-one—in order to make one as Himself. Here He mentioned His very own image and how His portrait, upright and marvelous, fitted clay, within which, by a divine breath, life could dwell—a wondrous element and a perfect fit for clay and spirit. It would be a soul.

Now the earth was at this time vacuously dark and had water intermixed with soil, and hot winds passed thick within the void. Hovering above, He began to curb the turbulent blend: light was the first to be made, which He split from the dark by shifting them to either day or night. Later on He made the sun and moon to keep the cycle of the light. So too, as He in His thoughts proposed, the mud was to be parted; the soil was heaped and girded by a substantial shore. On and around this land, it was now good to have all sorts of creatures form, quickened by His voice and by the template of their prototypes.

Dawn came, the sixth day, and He came down toward the clay, His wings folded from His hovering. He stooped, well-pleased, toward the clay, and there sprang forth the man by His molding hands. God rose, His thoughts happy toward the shape that stood like Him. Then passed a soft breath from God into the nostril of the clay, and God's dream woke and breathed the fruitful breath of God and the air of earth. This soul stirred before his God, and he checked himself as in a mirror, because as yet things were too new. Light soon rose within his soul, as might a hurried sun toward its midpoint role and there stop to beam all of its mighty light. Then Adam came to himself, and he knew God and felt his heart speed up in love to Him.

His body of clay was perfect and solid, but not so absolute or dense that it could hide the flame that burned inside. Soon the glory from within, from spirit deep, shone outward through its curtain and pulsed, and soft light surrounded all his manly form—godlike now, yet mild, in all things quite like a copy and very much a spark of God.

God prepared a garden for him, and God was here the gardener. He made an equal copy of another park, one in heaven, and styled it on the earth in Eden. He made it similar to the grand style of heaven and meant by this that loveliness should not rule this man; rather, beauty was subject to him, and heaven ought not any more impress. This visible matter was not created to be compared to heaven, as if it were a sort of black sheep of the stellar order. It was not meant for angels to look down upon, to tilt their heads and think of it disapprovingly, to think of it as a mutant sort of growth.

Adam, not a pilgrim yet, was placed within his paradise. He spontaneously knew it to be home. Adam rejoiced with virginal gaiety and crossed the garden, marveling. Now God was very pleased, and from His throne He leaned continually to watch the man, and every day God came down to walk this park. His heart was for the man. God never needed to walk too far because His steps were quickly heard and met; Adam would on a cross-path walk, and sometimes sprint, his legs obeying his love. So the two would meet and talk in friendly talk.

One day God said to Adam, "You seem in all good measures as the head of everything around. You know yourself to be superior, having seen the beasts and vegetation and compared and found yourself ahead. And this is for good reason, because I've built you so and made you excellent, and likewise I have bestowed authority with which to run the earth. See now that you use it wisely and in proportion to your stature. First off in your government, make a custom and give names and order to the animals, and also to the plants, that they may be called whatever you name them. And then, besides your tending of this paradise, spread out and view beyond the rivers; there are some wild plantations that are yet deformed. Your task is in subduing, and that not through concentrated labor, because you have your influence and by it can cast imbued words toward the land. You'll see the marshes dry up into a fountained park, and the moorlands too will follow this obedience. Also the seas, when you cross them in your flight, shall underneath you linger and tremble as if in dread."

Meanwhile, God saw that the man was alone, and He made Adam fall asleep through a soft caress, and He reached into his side to take a rib, to shape it into His own image. He held the rib in love outstretched and knit its parts into each other. God had thought this altogether neat, because He had thought of a future, of His own bride—who would in time be woven out of His own side, as by blood—the theme the same. The woman then was formed, and she stood up, her soul and form in glory equal to the man. She too was aflame with a surrounding light, and her limbs and features were perfect—one could say, divine. She was graceful first, then regal; Adam was regal first, then graceful. Her form was different from the man—her body cast as a shadow, a mimic of the structure of a soul—she had the capacity to hold a life within a life; whereas the man, his body masculine, retained in his flesh a copy of spirit that caused him to appear as life that could give life. In this way their conditions were quite marvelous—being the first parents of mankind and first in matrimony—wherein love was their sufficient tutor and desire. In this way they fared for many years: each day, love, and each day, honor, and each soft beat within their bosoms loud toward their God and toward each other. Out of heaven—it was not far away—many angels would appear to watch the happy pair, and they discerned in this a mystery, a secret that patience would reveal.

Satan also thought of this couple. He had become aware of them, because he had stolen unlicensed into heaven. Once he took himself up and made himself squat behind two sentinels, where he spied upon their speech and began to contemplate what he learned. A volatile anger seized him when he heard of earth and the two human beings. He first felt something of a jealousy, and then he felt he had a way to war with God through a war with man. He scurried down the spiral gate, his fury too impatient for a fluid glide, and made a course to earth.

What dreadful view to have seen for the first time the Dragon in his flight as he fast-winged flew through air and mist toward his prey. Satan had much desire to have an argument, to make strife against the pair, but he feared Adam and also Eve, as he knew them to have this world for their ministry, and he, an intruder, would beneath their rule be subject. A more pliant approach was needed. So thought he, the Devil: "I can't dote on Adam and Eve as I might with charm; they seem too much like God, too constant, too staunch. They would refuse my lure and prove me false, and more, perhaps, make me low, pride forbid, despising and chasing me around with ruling words or rods. Perhaps I could create a death, the strange thing that God mentioned a while back when He pressed the two and warned them of some tree. Since I can't bring them down directly, I'll choose this tree as my handy helper, a tree that I heard imbues persuasive knowledge of good and evil—and who knows what else. By means of this tree, I can make my scheme clandestine. I can bargain with them and put up this death for sale. What's the best way to seduce the pair? The man yearns toward the woman, and the woman seeks toward the man. I'll make use of that discrepancy; therein is device."

He ended his thought, which now looked for action. It required a false office, according to the model of deception—something that could make excuse for him even as he pretended through it. A cursory look around found a snake. It was walking unaware, and the order of snakes was not yet cursed to use their belly as a leg. Then Satan struck himself invisible, and he had his new carriage and a new mouth for his special use; he found it a good fit, that the snake was not contrary for him in its shape. The snake did not protest, it being feeble, and it climbed up into the bad tree, as by the urging of a subtle pulse and a certain voice inside its belly that exceeded its own sense. On an outstretched branch, the Devil waited, his host curled there, and he waited for Eve.

One day Eve came by to inspect the measure of the tree. She kept the matter to observation only, not daring to eat. She merely looked to ponder the fruit, to have by sight the force of view.

Satan struck, and the snake spoke Satan's whisper. "Are you the woman of the man and the good servant of God who lives above? I shouldn't wish to put a shame on this; no doubt you are with glory. You have your beauty, almost like an angel—in truth, so much like God. He is as a living fire, and you as a lower flame thereof. I see He visits you; I think it is for love. Perhaps that which He is also after is to give you a gentle persuasion, to see whether you, by your own will, can be shaped more into His likeness. He has made you in His image but with clay. Not that the clay would be an injury; it can't be that much a hindrance. At least, I don't think so. Strange, though, this dose of glory within the clay. I can't help but wonder if He privately means for you grow. Did God set this tree up here for nothing? Why is its fruit ambrosial and advertised? If I were you, I would make an inspection and reason out why He does not let you take of it. We know the tree has use for knowledge—and knowledge is always innocent—so I'd say to take of the crop and eat. Why grow halfway when you can grow complete?"

In this way the snake spoke, aloof, making a mixture with its words. Eve became confused. Her mind had swerved, with doubt between her thoughts, between the teaching of the snake and the far-off law of God. She thought a small bite to be enough, that therein was a compromise, that she could still pull back with wisdom's nearby thread.

She thought the sap sweet when new knowledge on her dawned; she felt not evil but was now aware of it—a strange feeling, a strange taste. She was rendered to wonder by this chance to look within the knowledge of both good and evil, to see their diverse possibilities, to see beyond the brightness of the light. She swam within these thoughts, a sort of bathing, a tending to awareness. She found therein no palpable fault. Why should one not in twilight sit, the moon to watch, and the sun? Each must round the other roll, for once light is formed, so too is its corresponding twin. East does fall into the long rim of its counterpart, the west. Only God—uncreated, invisible, and infinite—seemed to abide beyond this law.

After this she went to Adam to share her happy state, to tell him of the tree and of the promised death to those who took of it, which seemed now not at all so bad. But Adam was in despair. His heart was as no heart should be.

"My love, what has happened? I see a strange decaying in your works, some other color intermixed within your glow, a shadow that your body casts, a precursor of your death. Why did you crave for some other, when God and I were enough? Now I must take a quick view of things—your loss, which surely I couldn't stand, or our death combined, if I also of the robbing fruit would take. Oh, I wish I could think in general, but now I must be specific. Death seems patient and slow; there's more time for us to be in love. And what of God? Oh, my hurting heart is split! I think He'd love us still. Perhaps He has a way."

Adam took and ate the fruit deliberately—and wept. Soon afterward, God was in the garden, and He walked in the midst of the trees and called out to Adam and Eve. But fear impaired Adam, and he was slow to give account. At last he replied behind a grove, "I'm hiding behind this grove. I'm afraid of You because I'm naked. I've taken of the tree—my wife advised me to—and her advice wasn't hers either, but it was the snake who'd made temptation."

Then God replied, "The snake did wrong and has itself a curse. Also, it will have an enmity between My special Seed and it, and when the Seed in time through Eve's progeny will sprout, it will forever crush the serpent's head. Yet still the snake will give that Man, the Seed, the meanest bruise. From now on, the ground of the earth will behave differently, yielding thorns and other rebellious augments because of your sin. Adam and Eve, you've caused your own situation, as you've given up your authority. Sin is now over you, as is Satan, who took the keys of death and Hades. Indeed, Satan finds himself prince of this air. Now, before something worse happens to you, I must drive you out of Eden. If you were to take of the Tree of Life—which you've not yet done so far—and mix the two contrary fruits, the perpetual effect would be to cancel out your death, and you would live on without redemption, mixing life and death and bearing sickness evermore."

God then paused. His love looked for a solution, something that could answer sin, answer holiness, answer overrunning love. The first blood then was spilled, that of a deer. It was the first lesson by God of the consequence of sin and the way to approach a now unapproachable God. He took its hide to clothe them and to clothe their sin.

Chapter 4

— ❧ ✖ ❧ —

It was a strange thing to see Adam and Eve, once regal, run out of Eden with an unnatural run. Eden was against them and behind them, and for their sake two fierce cherubim were placed as guards at the entrance to the east. A flaming sword went spinning round and was meant to be offensive, lest the couple dare to think of a return.

Toward the second heaven, Satan flew. He called a council of the demons that were highly ranked to tell of success and of instigations.

"Our war with this God has a point. See how I have won this battle! There's a delectable discord between the race of man and God, and indeed I can now trade their lives. By my simple trick, I've procured their deaths through sin. Also, there's some other good news: we've obtained means to fly abroad, as I'm the earth's new prince. So let a group of us hurry up and on the earth begin our innate cures to employ and the place to infect; we have approval and consent. There's only one thing contrary to my success, a plan God has to turn man's scandal to success. Apparently a member of the race of man, at some future point, will in his actions correct me; the plan is for my head. Herein is anxiety, so let us be alert, and while we trouble earth with infestation, we keep an eye for his appearing and his stomping heel."

Meanwhile, Adam and Eve had, near the east of Eden, made camp, pondered their prospects, and checked out the land. The first night was long; they sleeplessly curled into each other, alert to the noisy, stricken beats of their hearts and the noise outside—new sounds coming from the opposing dark, sounds of nature growing under a curse, of yelps and roars from animals around. The beasts moaned as if they had against their former masters a great grief and a complaint.

The next day mankind's parents got up and discussed their state. "We've hidden ourselves too long. Despair almost found us out last night, but hope is free, we needn't conjure it. It's best we try to pause this death; it is like an angry steed, and we're on its back. It takes us dauntless to its cliff, our hand still on the bridle. Perhaps while it drives us so, we should drive it too, disturbing it with our good, neglecting neither our God nor purity. Death already has made us remote, our spirit dark as though it sleeps in stupor; no longer can it talk to God. Our bodies have had success in dominance, and they seem supreme; our flesh is the tie we have to somewhat of a life, an empty vessel through which we may yet look out for God. We can therefore by means of our flesh begin to work the land with labor and survive with sweat. Work will be our latest language and our binding law, our sacrifice, which might perhaps the murmur of our sins appease. God has shown us something in the slaying of the deer: that by the slaying of an animal for hide, its blood can work on our behalf. By this we'll take an example and have occasional sacrifice—to let His holiness be tolerant, to keep Him as our friend."

In this way, the two began to live. Children were added, who followed in this same principled way. Cain sprang from them first, his body like his father's, but his heart did seem apart. Satan had soon begun to measure Cain, to see if he was furnished for the promise, if he might be the one who would one day crush him. Satan watched as God advised Cain on his sin when he was less prudent and had less faith, when his fruits for God were burned in a lackadaisical mimic of a sacrifice, and when he got angry at his brother.

Satan also watched the second son and suspected him to be the Seed. That was Abel, who had by the blood of lambs and faith found the better way. Yet he lived not long within that way. His blood spoke from the ground, and his spirit cried when it in mourning lifted from his corpse and was then pulled downward toward a darker place.

Hades lapped him up; Abel's strength was not strong enough. There in Hades, Abel spoke. "My blood above speaks of my death. It calls for me to live; it calls for justice and for hope. It hopes more than I can hope. Am I forever now this dead creation, sealed up within the stomach of the earth? I'm dried up, my water in the soil. Oh, that I could've stayed a fountain-spring, a river made with all my being! Now I am in Hades stuck, and it differs little from a drought. I feel hindered; I feel all of sin on me imputed. My brother decided against me when he struck me with his deathblow. Yet I sense I'm not ended, that I'm not entirely discharged from the living, that there's something to discover within God. I can't quite think it out right now; I think it's concealed. I will with one eye weep out all my packed-up tears and with the other stare out much to God. This Hades is for me no teacher. I'll keep it not as my eternal hope."

God saw the vice of Cain, for Abel's blood had called to Him, saying that he was no longer. And God gazed within the depths of Hades and saw Abel there and heard his grief. Then God went down to Hades and comforted Abel. "I've heard your outcry and know that you're shut within this dark place. Hades has its gate and is himself Death's conjoint twin. For the time being, you are his prey. He has practiced first on you, and soon others will be for his hungry mouth. Your blood calls out for justice; it's incessant in My ears. I'll have My justice and my trial when I, by My own arm, will gather all of sin as in a single basket, and then I will judge the basket and cast Him out, even to this very place. Wait for the One on whom My wrath will pour; therein is your life and actual hope."

Meanwhile, mankind began to multiply and, besides this, lived very long. Adam himself grew old and reached nine hundred and thirty years. The Spirit had still hovered then, correcting in some way mankind's years, even as their sins continuously would appoint their deaths.

Satan too had roamed around; he had not hoped for reproduction and was perplexed by mankind's fertile state. He had sat, sad-faced, in a meditating pose and thought of human bodies, of genetics, of how they could outlive his death by birth, of how the laws of earth were laws for him as well. After brooding on the circumstance and his own head, which was in jeopardy, he came up with a plan to change the scales unevenly, to mitigate the Seed who would against him sprout with sword-like aim. The plan was to defile the offspring, to graft a foreign seed into the genes of man in order to succeed against the Seed by making chaos through congenital mixture.

Now it happened around the same time that God was very conscious of mankind and did as much as He could to approach them. When mankind began to be more impaired by the darkness of their minds and futility, He sent two hundred watcher angels down to earth. These angels were conspicuous in their knowledge and desire to help mankind. From this institute of guidance came much good, at least at first. Who knows how, exactly—whether it was Satan's charm or the fatigues of living among stubborn men—but a temptation started crowding out the exclusive and holy focus of the angels on the ground. When the thought became overpowering, they gathered together and conspired to comply with the temptation of lust. Their leader Azazel said to them, "We're of unequal accountability, as I am your head, and I wonder, if we do this temptation, whether you'll all blame it on me."

The other angels answered, "On the contrary, we'll make a pact and be in this together."

The mode of their spirit form was expanded beyond its boundary, and a shape of flesh was borrowed in place of the flame of light. In their temptation, they thought this crossover to be an advantage, as now the two hundred angels could solidly confirm themselves and their bodies to be familiar with flesh, with the daughters of men. After a while, when these freshly fallen watcher angels came to some sense and knew they could not hide the pleasantness of mating with the human women or the rudeness of their offense against God, they went to Enoch, a faithful man and descendent of Adam, and asked him to add an attachment to his prayer to God, a plea for a merciful deal.

No deal was found. There was no way for them to wash or rebirth, for they had gone further than the limits of rescue. An indignant archangel was consequently sent from heaven, who scooped up the two hundred and bound them in Tartarus, where they would hang upside down even up to the present day.

Indeed, something awful had now been admitted into earth and into the race of men. When the angels had had intercourse with the women, their pleasure had not only been in the act but in the hope of offspring. By this means and propagation passed into existence the notorious Nephilim, the hybrids—half-angel, half-man. And so Satan sent mankind this evil thing, a tampered gene. Giants rose from this perversion. They roamed the earth and took from man what they could take. Violence was within this hybrid scourge, a horrid breed! The giants—that is, the Nephilim—did whatever they wished with their superior intellect and corpulent animation. Some of them were recklessly abandoned to violence and made further flexures in sin through the invention of cannibalism and the teaching of sorcery. Some of the more prudent Nephilim, who were in the mood for rest rather than a laborious war with puny men or each other, used wit and consultation, teachings of astronomy and astrology, to subdue an irritated mankind placidly to their will. Religious designs were shrewdly fitted for the scheme, and a faith was formed around these demi-gods.

In time (and this went on for a thousand years or so) the patience of God had run out. He had had enough. He was grieved that so much had been done and that mankind had shunned His sweetness. From His wisdom and His grief came the thought to dim the light, to end their cause and blot them out.

Now there was one man left on earth who was, as compared to his peers, peculiar, and to God in particular, because his genes were yet pure, undefiled by the encroaching bad seed of the hybrids that had mixed in with all other genealogies of mankind. The love of God reveled in this man Noah; and there was still a probability that He would save him.

One day God called Noah and said to him, "Assuredly, it's a mess, and I'll have to wipe mankind off the face of the earth. However, you have the benefit of time to run ahead of My big storm. I've kindled it already, making it to churn. Make now an escape, a ship that can above My swipe and all My waters drift: an ark that will save you and your family."

God watched as Noah did as He had advised. In time, Noah and his family entered into the ark, and a collection of animals and birds, male and female of each type, went inside as well, and from behind, God shut the door with His finger.

In all the days of earth, no one had seen or heard of rain; the soil as yet had drunk the dew or sipped from nearby fountain streams. Who knows exactly how? Perhaps it was true that the earth had a canopy and that the sky had soft clouds beneath a matrix of hydrogen that suppressed the rain within that crystal bubble. Noah's peers indeed could not imagine a flood. They idly thought of Noah's admonition, of his warning that water could be potent.

Perhaps from the stars of Orion it moved. It sailed so magically, it seemed to glide. It had swum so through the stars as might a water snake among the lilies of a pond, when it then fixed its cold eye forward and senselessly turned, and its tail began to waft toward the planet earth. Jupiter was too slow; it was at the far-off end of its circle. It tried to catch the rock but could not crosswise leap to pull it with its gravity. It is to be conceived, if one regards the heavy rock, that doom came fast. The earth's crown was crust; a crust that lost cohesiveness. Gravity began to vex the windows of the sky; they had no shoulders whereon to hang. And so the floodgates opened and the fountains were unstopped, the pressure less, as there was no longer downward force to manage them. Can one hate water as much as mankind did when they boldly opposed and tried to fight the warbling streams?

It rolled over them quickly, and almost all of mankind was dead—were it not for Noah's ark, which made up mankind's hope. Satan had begun to flatter himself over this; he was taken up by this great flood, by all the death. He called himself great, saying that he could crown the earth with death, that he could invoke God's wrath for man. Satan flew back to the second heaven where he recalled his cohorts and there them summoned for a speech.

"See now how I had God's arm behind Him turned, even to give the race of man a proper death. It argues to what way we can bend His will, so that when the remnant multiply, I shall again stoke them with my violence."

Months went by, and the ark at length stopped on a mountain and stayed there, disabled. The little family trooped outside and on the ground walked strangely, kissing it in prayer, bending low that they might reach full gratitude. Also, there was a special sacrifice—Noah's doing—of those animals that were in sevens brought, by which God was pleased, not because of their deaths but because their blood could serially cover man's sin.

God had on all of this reflected and felt sympathy. Accordingly, He shaped a rainbow in the air—such light had hung before above the throne—a fit sign for His promise that hereafter there would never be a flood like this again, and there would be from now on seasons to fashion out the heat and cold, and in this cycle there would be time for seeds and time for harvests.

Chapter 5

—— ⋅⊰ ✖ ⊱⋅ ——

Mankind again began to rise, trading and multiplying and doing what was common. When they traveled east, they found a suitable flat landscape. There they imagined stairs upward, so high they might reach heaven. They spoke to each other, and their language was the same.

"Let's be toward each other equal, tend our condition, make our name great, and build a high tower, such that we may always have escape. We can achieve such height!"

God saw their building and went down to inspect. He walked around and saw that they by their strength had excused Him; technology and ambition had privilege.

"They seek to make a cure and a false success. If they achieve this, what will stop them and what will become of them? They prefer the strength of intellect, of flesh, over the treasures of the spirit. If they can run so far in unity, in the fineness of their minds, what else will they contrive? They may, in ignorance, find a way out of redemption."

So God considered the basis of their unity and made their language clash. Since then they could not quite understand or realize each other, they began to seem erroneous to each other. In time, groups of peoples started to form, and each to his own faction said, "In our hour of success, we've failed. Who thought words could oppose us, that words could make our single cause multiple?

Why learn another tongue when all their words seem deviant. It's better then to move our tribe; the earth is big enough."

Around that same time, Nimrod, descendent of Noah, had risen as leader of mankind. His stately ascendance came by the hard condition of violence; he was a predator, and he hunted men. His notorious career was fearfully applauded by a fearful people. His violence was commanded by his carnal lusts and amplified under the shadow of a remarkable condition: some genetic code had been reactivated. Perhaps it came through the sin of Ham or through a dormant hybrid trait that had passed on from Noah's wife. Who knows? And the traits of the giants that were thought extinct or exhausted because of the flood slowly resurfaced in this man's body. And so he began to be a Nephilim.

Under the weight of time and posterity, Nimrod's legend was buried in the coffins of myth and in the names of Apollo, Osiris, or perhaps even Zeus, as well as others. What Nimrod began at the tower of Babel—that is, the teaching of rebellion, the teaching of idolatry—was nursed into a new religious mindset and grown figuratively into the spiritual and mysterious city of Babylon, which earned the expressive appellation: "Babylon the great, the mother of all harlots and of the abominations of the earth." The people lamented Nimrod's death, but the scrolls of the past and even a few Scriptures are pregnant with, or at least suggestive of, the theme of his resurrection at the end of the age: the wound of death would be healed, and an astonished end-time people would welcome the return of their valiant antichrist.

Meanwhile, mankind spread, each to his own design, looking forward and despising the past, neglecting the lesson of the flood. In due time, their spiritual—or rather carnal—designs did yield their crop: a harvest full of fluff and fancy ways of worship, each tribe keeping some rudiments of old times, or at least some sense of deity, as much as their flesh would permit. In the course of their degeneration, new priests or clerics of some sort broke out and, with their left hand, pride-wise, made strange rules, some invoking sacrifice, as it seemed a humble thing to do. Their right hand vainly pointed upward, as though to point through the mists toward some far-off truth that there was a far-off God—or gods, perhaps—who had His life—or lives—far off, and that the steady pace of ritual and worship might perhaps charm the distant god's hand into a blessing.

So then there was Abram, far-off descendent of Noah, who lived in this mystical time and saw something in the moon and expected it to grant him a blessing.

One can probably grant that the moon is a noble light, though one would think it better to choose the sun, as it seems to be the stronger player in the scales of fate. Nonetheless, Abram was a moon-worshipper, but not for long. The time came for Abram to feel through the night and past the beam of the moon to something further, something true.

One black night, when Abram was lulled with wine and moon, God came to his side. God disturbed the pause that had subdued Abram's heart and picked him for blessing, but not some ordinary blessing. It was the kind that would supersede all others and was in its range so much that it created a new disposition. A new thing had begun on earth, and the strays, the pitied tribes of man, would now be able to discern a better shape beyond the misty shapes of lesser gods. The truth of God, His existence, would be reintroduced by Abram in a shape clearer than the conjured spirits of old gods—those spirits whom the pagan priests had to pilot through the stars when they worshipped a starlit sky, or those spirits whom the cleric had to bring from the spirit side or from the zone of death by witchery or some weird maneuver into the realm of man.

A true blessing now was in place for all mankind through Abram. Now God had made His plan, His ambition to save mankind, that He might draw them back to light. First, then, came assurances to Abram, who asked God how the blessing He had promised could be possible, and by what means. It would be by the forming of an agreement, a covenant. Animals would be cleaved in two, and by God and Abram walking through the blood of all the halves, a covenant bond would be durably confirmed.

When Abram had set the halves of the animals, split on each side, he waited for God's arrival. But he fell asleep in a sort of trance and saw dark things and wonders ahead. Meanwhile God appeared as a fire like an oven ablaze. Abram saw God walk His turn through the blood. Abram's turn was next to walk between the animal halves, but he was in a trance asleep and could not walk. He saw another blaze—he saw it in his sleep—and instead of oven heat, there was a torch, and the second part of God Himself walked through the halves on Abram's behalf. God had done this on purpose and mysteriously, and at the time He did not light the plan too brightly; He would in patience and in kindness slowly fold out the plan.

In time, God added to the blessing included in the covenant for Abram and for his seed forever. And Abram, now Abraham, received more promise of a deeper blessing and blood again—by circumcision this time around—as blood was required for God to approach. How else could God's justice be suppressed? Only blood, then, could fetch proximity, according as His holiness allowed.

It was not that God thought less of blood. In fact, it was the only thing that had value enough to cover uncoverable sin. Let the critic be mute.

Will Job speak to mankind to help them out in their confusion? There was a day before Abraham's blessing, during the time of Job, when the angels came to God. It was a meeting of some sort with the angels in their varied kinds. Then, within the midst of the angelic bloom in heaven, a strange noise barked with echoing effusion. Close from behind, a villain presented among the sons of God. Satan had himself dropped by, the holy chorus to disrupt. What did he do but make a deliberate nuisance of himself, as his pride was hurt when God had called the sons and not included him. Then God saw Satan and said to him, "What have you been up to? Give an account."

Satan answered, "Not up to much. I'm rather bored. I have my jaded strolls around the earth."

God spoke again to Satan. "And what of Job? Have you taken note of him, how he steers himself away from you? You think it's my hedge around him that lets him be so good, that if there was no hedge, then there would be no goodness either. It's true that he suppresses your evil by My hedge, but he too suppresses the hedge by his fear."

Afterward, Satan flew down to earth and saw this thing, and he noted how he could obtain advantage, thereby to break Job's goodness. Satan observed Job for a while and looked around the protective hedge for holes. Little time elapsed before Satan found his spot and made Job lose his family and his fortune. Then Job's friends came to comfort him, to help Job's grief through reason.

They each could match Job's loss by way of wisdom—their own wisdom that they smeared on Job, heavy oracles of vanity. They wished to turn Job to their tide, but Job was prickly and did not wish to move. This made the friends unpleasant, and their oracles also turned in a way that made Job more at fault and summarized and shaped God as though they were His equal. But Job labored underneath all of this and did not sin, nor did he accuse God but rather turned more toward God. God at length stepped into the conversation. He presented in a whirlwind, spinning therein for the visual benefit of natural flesh.

He spoke to Job. "Your friends are at fault in finding fault. They think they hit it right when they handily describe My virtue and make their judgment and reason equal to mine. They make My judgment such a force, and they arm Me, so they think, with arms of wrath. Justice is as a scepter at My left, but at My right, My mercy assists. Your friends can't discern between the two, nor even understand lesser things such as the ways of nature—and you too are beneath the reach of it."

Job then withdrew his questions, as he was aware of his own rank. Job said to God, "I'll pause here. I don't have Your height. I now know I can't give you counsel, and though it's proper enough to give gratitude and praise, I'll speak one more thing. It's clear to me—I understand and hope it'll be so one day—that mankind gets a go-between, one who fits Your size and mine."

God subsequently made Job to prosper even more and doubled all his ways.

One sunny day, Abraham sat at the oaks of Mamre in the welcome shadow of his tent. He had sat at the entry of his tent, heated and contently dazed, when he looked up, peering far into the wideness of the daylight, and saw three men walking past. They came in lesser majesty than what they could have. They looked natural, like physical men, yet there was something in their shape, a heavenly residue that Abraham recognized, a glory that burned within them. God had come for a look with two angels at His side. Abraham quickly ran to intercept them, pleading with them to linger and spend some time in the shade of the nearby tree for the sake of food and drink, which he scurried off to prepare.

God honored this. He and the two angels took the food and drink. There were a choice calf, bread cakes, curds, and milk— the finest that Abraham had. Afterward, God told Abraham of his future son Isaac who would rise from Sarah. Mankind's blessing—God's Seed—would come through this lineage.

Now God and the two angels were on their way, and Abraham walked along to send them off. It must have been nice and sweet to walk with God, but for God it was a sweetness mixed, because He had thought of something else. As they walked, and at length, God revealed to Abraham His particular concern. "For your sake, I say this, that Sodom and Gomorrah are to be taken by My wrath. I've rated it doomed, because their wickedness has been brimming over with a bloodlust, an intentness and industry that can no more be considered with leniency. Their day has come. Wiles come too easily for them, and they lay their hands to far worse, and are altogether exceedingly wicked. Who will intercede for them? They have as of yet no intercessor."

Then Abraham said to God, "It's not for nothing that You're just. I know You by now, that You can't do things false.

Therefore, what if fifty righteous people were to be found in the cities? Does doom have such an awful permit? And what if—allow my dust to speak—what if there were only forty? Would they elude that doom? What then of thirty—I go now on presumption. Would thirty righteous forbid their fate? I'll hold my words now after this—I press You only by our covenant, which has made me bold—whether ten might lend what twenty cannot borrow?"

One wonders what would have happened if Abraham had in that notion gone further. Perhaps he had paused too soon; perhaps he had prejudged God up to ten or thought that ten righteous people would no doubt be found amongst the thousands of Sodom and Gomorrah.

Then God lifted Himself to heaven, and the two angels went on to Sodom, there to look, to count to ten, if they could reach that high. But the two cities were lacking, and it became a matter of great commotion, as in the meanwhile, the angels stayed at Lot's house, there to have respite for the night.

The men of the city were out and about, roaming around, and the vices of that infamous people produced an awful offense. They had noticed the two angels in town, and they burned in lust toward them. Perhaps they assumed them to be men, and strangers. Eager evil forced its way, as the men wished to abuse the angels. But the men could not drag the angels out of the house, because the angels made the men fall into a sort of stupor, and in consequence they searched for the door without discovery. Their eyes were dimmed so that they could not find what they felt for. At length the impatient angels grabbed the too-patient Lot by the hand—he needed this encouragement—along with his wife and two daughters and pressed them to hurry up and flee.

The fame of Lot's wife is known; she died when her ambition for her past, in its last struggle, made her turn back to look at the city. She was not altogether sure about all the fuss, and her speed was too slow, and her body transformed into a salty pillar when the flames came down.

Chapter 6

————— ❧ ✖ ❧ —————

God had His entire interest in mankind, but He was unable to bless them in the full terms of His love and His wish. The only way to connect with them was by means of an agreement, a covenant, so that He had a better footing into a domain that belonged to man and the air that belonged to Satan. All of this was because the lords of the earth, mankind, were standing under sin, and Satan, the overarching lord of sin, was standing by. God is a landlord, so to speak, who recognizes His lease with the distinction and eye of a principled judge. Mankind had been given a dominion that had an unfortunate success over the omnipotence of God. God therefore regained entrance by means of a covenant—in this case, with Abraham—whereby God could bless and eventually offer redemption for all mankind through him. This is the importance of Abraham.

One can hardly imagine God's patience. A lesser being's patience would have expired if he'd had to hold his love in silence because his bride was playing deaf and hard-to-get. But God had patience and kindness, and He went on while no one saw. Therefore He wished to fine-tune His covenant with Abraham to give Himself more room, and that by Abraham's consent. In the process, and at that very moment in a far-off time, He leaned across all heaven and called again to him.

God's peculiar request gives pause, and a sensible person is baffled in search of the cogent motive, as the request contained instructions filled with grief. If grief could bleed, it would have bled all out. God asked Abraham for his son Isaac, the one through whom the Seed would come. He called for Isaac's life—by sacrifice. Abraham was to slay his only son.

Abraham assumed far more than the average person would. He believed that God would raise the slain son to life again and so make descendants and keep His promise through resurrection. To the mountain Abraham went with his young son, and Isaac was unaware. But God was too good to have Abraham's heart all wrecked. He stopped him, even with the knife in hand, and said to Abraham, "There is no longer need. There is a substitute instead, a ram stuck in the briar bush. Take it in your son's place."

This dark deed was then full of light. By Abraham's faith had the covenant expanded, grown by its magnificence. In consequence, God—who had to continually maneuver through the allowances of man and his covenants—could now bless all the more, and by the terms of the covenant, yield His own Son also in time. He had obtained the bolstered right.

Isaac grew up, and the blessing was with him. When Isaac became a man, God sent His angel ahead to Mesopotamia. He had in mind a wife for him: Rebecca. She was not a Canaanite; she was of the old house of Abraham. God had done this deliberately, because in her would be the expectation of descendants. The heritage could not be diluted, nor ought there to be any chance of contamination by the wild strain of the Nephilim.

Two nations were within Rebecca's womb, twins who strove against each other: Esau, first and firstborn, and Jacob next, who held the heel of Esau when he passed by in birth. Esau was first as well in wildness; he did not care and was casual when he took two mean wives for himself. Their meanness became evident when they spurned Rebecca. Esau was also blithe when he recklessly sold to Jacob his rights of the blessing of the firstborn—for a pot of soup.

Rebecca had had enough of her pestering daughters-in-law, and she swayed Jacob to trick his blind father by playing the firstborn son. The smell of the field upon Esau, the hunter, was faked through Esau's clothes, and an old goatskin on Jacob's neck mimicked Esau's hairy neck. So Jacob committed a fraud, whereby obtaining the firstborn's blessing, and his father's blindness was derided.

One is disturbed by this. One wants it to be better. One wonders why mankind's past and present have this philosophy, why mankind's ways are dark and midnight long. With the spirit dark, the soul clings to notions of morality. She, the soul, swerves a bit when she seeks toward her truths; she needs a consolation. She stirs halfheartedly, needing something definite in the emptiness that might give her order. She strives to find a moral code by incidental quest, to have the common sight of common man; safety in the herd. It is her gamble and her doctrine to side with the masses and hope for the best. Indeed, the past shines dark on humanity's back, and its destined dawn is as a setting sun.

Meanwhile, Jacob became an adult and moved out. He went to work for a man called Laban, taking care of his sheep. Laban, Jacob's uncle, looked down on him and exploited him when he could. Jacob received for his wages all the spotted sheep and goats that were born, and his uncle Laban had for himself all the white ones because there were more of them.

Now this Laban was devious and had the few spotted animals separated from his flock of whites, and he had them divided by a three-day walk. In spite of the hard conditions of the unfair scheme, Jacob forced the blessing of God onto the white herd by a peculiar mechanism. He carved sticks in a spotted fashion to resemble a spotted lamb and displayed them before the herds whenever they would go to the troughs to drink. Jacob presumed that the ignorant and reposing herd would obtain an insensible hint by this and mimic the carved bark in their offspring.

Whether the bark indeed transfused such magic is unknown. More likely, knowing the workings of the blessing, it was Jacob's faith, discharging effectively through a highly visual scheme, that did the fertile work of the imitation.

Jacob worked for Laban for several years. It was for love, because his heart was fast for Rachel, Laban's daughter. Laban, the old schemer, tried to use this to keep Jacob as his worker. He would give Rachel to Jacob after seven years' service. Jacob's heart beat faster than the slow beat of seven years of waiting. When the time came for the marriage, Laban's other daughter, Lea, was substituted under the veil. Jacob's surprise, when he had lifted the veil, was quietly lamented and perhaps disguised. He took Lea in and worked another seven years to fulfill the vile barter and obtain Rachel from Laban's hand. Afterward, Jacob and his families sought out other lands, and he left with his caravan and wealth.

God met Jacob on his trip. One night while Jacob slept, there were the workings of a dream. A visitor appeared and obstructed the advancing dreamy path. It must be a strange thing to find a *live* man within the common specters of one's sleep, among the forms and shapes that hide from the daytime, preferring nighttime's side, and collect themselves as if they have the right to tell their stories while one sleeps. Jacob had the interrupting man in sight and instantly saw that the man was not indigenous; he had a different aura, something solid that did not gather like the rest in hazy, random drifts. He reckoned right that it might be God, who angel-like had produced Himself within the dream.

Jacob felt sure of something about this Man, and by the measure of his certainty, he nagged the Man to give him more in blessing. Jacob must have connected the stories of his father, Abraham, to his daring and familiar interaction with God. Jacob did not wish for a mere oracle; he troubled God as though he could prevail. The two wrestled the whole night, and in the end, Jacob came out of it with a perpetual limp in his gait. God had touched his walk and changed his name to Israel, meaning "prince of God." Perhaps Jacob took his new name with the sincerity of devotion, but however he took it, it became prophetic and perpetually expressive of a people who would destined to wrestle with God.

Twelve sons were born to Jacob, of whom the name and person of Joseph stands out for notice. Joseph's life had a noble course, an integrity that endured, a life that carried prophetic strains of what was to come in the promised Seed. Joseph was loved by his father Jacob, but his brothers held him to a variety of spurning. And when Joseph told his brothers of his dreams wherein he would be lifted high above them, they despised him and threw him to the misery of a pit, smearing his robe with blood in order to make to their father believe he was dead.

Their hands had more than fraud in mind, and they actually would have killed him, had not Reuben, the oldest son, stopped their next deed with his advice that the pit would better manage their hate. Meanwhile, Reuben had in himself devised to afterward part ways with the others' abhorrence and steal Joseph at night and secretly from the deep. When Reuben returned with this intent, he did not find his brother, because by chance a caravan of traders had passed by and had taken Joseph with them.

Joseph's tears were now those of a slave. Yet God had pity and moved against this bad deed. The caravan and Joseph ended up in Egypt, where Joseph at length started working for Potiphar, a captain of the Pharaoh's guard. Stagnation is the typical vector of bondage, but there was something in the spirit of Joseph that opposed or overruled the conditions necessary for that kind of recession. And in time, Joseph was conferred over all of Potiphar's house.

In the moment of a happy promotion, when all the dreams and hopes are of a common mind, another force sometimes appears. In this case and in this nice house, it was Potiphar's wife who made an exploit. Flesh rushed in on her one day when she saw the dashing Joseph alone. She spoke charmingly to him, but her warmth quickly turned to anger, because he had dismissed her advances.

Pride will defend itself, no matter what, and one wonders what is so precious about it to build such massive walls. Behind pride's door a weakness waits. At any rate, Potiphar's wife's felt something like pain, and she called aloud, pretending to need help.

She called him offensive and accused him of attempted rape. Grief again came for Joseph, as the sweeping tide of life turned into a storm and threw him into jail, where he sat for years, perplexed. He must have answered self-pity with his faith, and he must have answered well, because self-pity can thrive in pain. God's voice was still the voice in him, and the blessing blessed him in jail, despite what was around him, and raised him up as head of that scene.

Now the chief baker and the chief cupbearer of Pharaoh were also imprisoned there. The irritated and sovereign mood of the Pharaoh had no doubt something to do with their incarceration. One night, while in jail, both of these men had a dream. The dreams confounded them both, and an interpretation by Joseph projected symbolism into their actual sense: one would be hanged in three days and the other raised again to serve before Pharaoh. When Joseph gave the good news to the cupbearer, he asked him to remember him when all was well. Joseph's interpretation was fulfilled, but the cupbearer, restored to Pharaoh's house, at once forgot about Joseph in the jail, and Joseph's plea was eclipsed by the indifference of this complacent man.

However, another dream was at work, this time within the mind of Pharaoh. It was not the workings of a happy mind in happy sleep. In Pharaoh's mind, seven fat cows performed for the sake of the dream. These cows climbed up from the banks of the Nile and fed of the lush marshes. Seven more cows played in this theater. These ones, lean and worn, came after and ate the fat cows; yet with all their eating, they remained lean and worn. A second dream after the same fashion came to Pharaoh in the same night: seven ears of grain swayed plump to make the same point. These were then overgrown and surpassed by seven withered ears of grain.

The dream was told to Pharaoh's magicians to have them interpret it. Regardless of the magicians' eager intent, the dream kept its secret to itself, and they could not resolve the pictures. It happened that the cupbearer found himself within this junction; he swallowed his pride and related the shame of his time in the dungeon, where a Hebrew youth was still confined. He told the Pharaoh that this young man had something different about him, that he could with wise contemplations weave the threads of dreams together.

Pharaoh consequently had Joseph washed and dressed and introduced into his court. Joseph relayed the thing—how the cows and ears spoke in terms of years of wealth and want, respectively. In this way, Joseph taught the Pharaoh how his dream was possible, and in wisdom he spoke of the advantage of detaining from the first seven years of overflow some portions, which would have an effect, over time, in the years of famine, such that the land could outlive the lack. Pharaoh had an effusion of wonder and regard for Joseph and appointed him to the lofty position of head over all of Egypt, second only to Pharaoh himself.

After seven years, the dream's second side unfolded. These were the years of famine, and from Canaan, Joseph's brothers came to Egypt looking for food. They bowed before Joseph, not knowing him, and when he revealed himself to them—his virtue had allowed for the forgiveness of his conniving brothers—he poured his heart out in tears. His dumbfounded brothers eventually came to their senses and repented and embraced him with bewailing sobs.

Chapter 7

— ❖ —

Four hundred years went by, and new rulers took the sovereign seat in Egypt. A new Pharaoh inferred that the Israelites, who had grown in number, would soon hamper the progressive career of the Egyptians. He therefore started showing them the upper hand. However, even under this oppressive lash, the Israelites kept on increasing.

Now Satan had taught murder early, and he wished here to revive it to a grand scale. He understood the danger of the Israelites with their covenant. Perhaps Satan suspected that the Seed would come through their lineage. The trick was to hide the murder in a better form. This time around, he urged the Pharaoh on by fear, letting him think in terms of mathematics and perceive a fatal number in the numerous. And indeed it was fatal for many newborn sons who were ordered to be drowned in the Nile. The murders meant, for Satan, a chance to kill the Seed.

Satan had a hunch about the birth of someone great, the rising of a son of man. Moses entered the scene, gliding in a basket on the Nile; his parents, with desperate tears, had concealed him in this way and sent him drifting off. Pharaoh's daughter happened to be basking next to the Nile, and her glance of wonder and sympathy saved Moses from the murderous edict of her father. The child was taken in by her, and his own mother was given to him as a nursemaid, Pharaoh and his daughter being unaware of this delightful fortuity.

Moses grew up under the partial sanction of the royal courts, but his Hebrew blood influenced his loyalties. His loneliness was equal to all his luxury, and he saw the Egyptian riches as gross and a truer prize in Israel. In time his soft robes could not disguise his hard thoughts, which were lit up by his passion for his own people. One day he slew an Egyptian for beating a Hebrew in the field. Pharaoh heard of this and took it contemptuously; his prejudice went farther than his mercy, and he sought to kill Moses.

Moses won his life through speed, and he fled without conscious aim toward a well at Midian. At the well he sat, his hope sour, and he did not know which way to go. Then seven young women came to the well to water their father's flock. There were other shepherds too at the well, who for their own ease had made the women wait until they were finished. Under the necessity of fairness, Moses stood up and interfered for the women's sake. Afterward, when the women's father heard of the chivalry of the man at the well, he called for Moses and made him his foreman and, in time, his son-in-law.

The course of Moses' life had changed, and for many years it was suspended by the tending of flocks. Whatever happened during those years is unclear, yet the shepherd's troughs, rather than the royal tables, must have taught him something and impressed upon him a more vital way of life.

One day he took the flock of sheep westward to Horeb, the mount of God. It was just another day wherein time grew large, its pace the slow pace of perhaps boredom or despondency, but then his vacant gaze had its subject changed: he saw a burning bush. It began for him as a curiosity, and he walked toward it to ascertain the strange thing. Fear overcame curiosity when the flame did not consume the bush but instead called out his name in confidence. Then he understood that the phenomenon was urged on by something supernatural.

God proposed His plan to Moses through the burning bush. God had in this way made a passage to earth, as He could not otherwise engage with man. Abraham's covenant was His constraint and his right to have dealings with mankind. Again, though He was the Lord of the earth and in desperate mood to help humanity, He did not have the right to willfully impose His love and pleasure. When He had given earth to mankind, along with eminent independence of heart and will, He could not take it back, even when the earth laid slave to man and man to sin. Therefore, God had Himself entangled with covenants; this was the only way to elbow in, to get His footing—through the will of man.

God needed more, needed someone, and in this case He needed Moses. By way of a command introduced as a request, He chose Moses to be His instrument of permission. This peculiar tenet may seem objectionable and apparently paradoxical to His omnipotence. Still, in truth, neither are rejected: omnipotence is confined by integrity. And when God revealed Himself to Moses, Moses took off his sandals and hid his face from the frightening blaze. Moses would become God's minister. He was to go back to Egypt and set His people free.

Moses and his family packed up and took the long road to Egypt. It happened as if there were a duplicity in the workings of God. God waited for a dispute on the road in the path of the caravan, and He was ready to kill Moses whom He had just assigned.

Moses' wife, Zipporah, who had the right mind and clue, saved his life. She was quick to unwork the danger, and she circumcised her son to prevent the touch of God by blood. The implacable holiness of God was tempered by blood. Still the repetitive blood of circumcision or animals only tried the mercy of God. It could never fully gratify the demands of holiness, could never boast or reach to the forgiveness of sin, and always caused man to approach God at a distance. The argument made by blood had validity only in that it was attached to the blood of the Seed;

His blood was the only recognized and brave ministry that could impute full forgiveness and absolute access to God. And in this scenario with Moses, God's holiness tolerated Moses inasmuch as God was seeing something father off—the sight of the perfect blood of the perfect Lamb.

At this time in history, Israel and Moses tottered still under the shade of future things, they had their motions in an ancient echo from the future. Does it not say that the Lamb was slain before the foundations of the earth? It was for this reason also that God deemed the blood of lambs of value on the doorposts of the houses of the tribes, when He, through the inflexible hand of the angels of judgment, passed over the doors on the Passover before leading His people out of Egypt.

Now God had not reduced redemption solely to the Jews, and though He seemed to circle here around the tribe like a hen who gathers all her chicks, He in fact flew farther in His plan, eagle-like, and wished life for all mankind. But at this junction, darkness reigned on all mankind, and God reigned through Israel. Meanwhile, Moses had by plagues made bitter the land and hearts of Egypt, and at length the distraught Pharaoh had allowed the people to go.

When Israel was finally out there in the wilderness on the way to the Promised Land, God sent them the long way, because He was concerned that they would be frightened of what was to come by seeing wars going on within their future land, that they might be persuaded to the return to the familiarity and safety of bondage.

It came about—as Israel was roaming about—that God came to the earth. On the mount of Sinai He alighted within a flame of fire, a fire fatal for the mount, which could not lie still nor do less than burn in smoke and quakes. And God was careful for His people and warned them to look away, because their flesh in sin would be burned because of the closeness of the approach of God. With respect to the thunders and quakes, the fumes and fires, it was not that God was in the mood to scare the people or to break forth on them or to make a dreadful figure of Himself unnecessarily. No, He would have been very glad to stretch Himself out in love and have a tender meeting and have His arms all wide. Yet He had only one standard: the standard of perfection.

Flames do not sleep as water may, and God was aflame upon the mount, busy making law. First came the Ten Commandments, the general ordinances for mankind, a plumb line, as it were, that might drop down on the heart of man. It was the pulse for all the rest that would in time beat in more sundry and severer laws. Whatever slant of enmity might have been suggested by the law of Moses, it really was meant for blessing. , Nonetheless, the latitude within the Law itself forced a duty of obedience and labor which no common person was able to follow. God was aware of this when He made all the laws. He had no wish for the law to outlive man. If there were any bold tyranny in the Law, its heat and flames were burning hot for sin, not man. Sin, as a construct, has a slippery shape, and indeed cannot be intercepted or grasped by a limp-wristed hand.

The Law, then, was to give sin a finish. The Law looked eagerly for sin; it was the hook, the bait, the strong hand that could clasp sin tight. And sin meanwhile had drawn toward the law and found itself not quite undone; it sat in comfort next to the Law. Sin watched the wide scope of the Law fashion out its prey, because the Law, though good, gave sin its strength. It gave sin what it had sought and God what He had hoped. God had woven the Law as one would weave a basket, and a basket, it is assumed, is not without the thing inside. By a brilliant move, God would, in a special Man, satisfy the entire Law and do away with sin, as sin was contained in the Law.

Israel, during this time and in consequence, tried to work out in pity their obedience toward the Law, which did not pity them back. Among many things, the Law informed them of the Sabbath to correct their rest by coercion. At a distance, the Sabbath casts a shadowy, bullying figure, as do the outgrowths of all the sundry laws. Yet if there is any shadow from the Sabbath, it ought to be seen as the salutary and cheerful forecast of the end of all works, of grace and rest.

There is something else that hangs mute upon the Law of the Sabbath, something that attributes to God's reputation that He somehow rested on the seventh day because He was tired. In fact, God helps out and rejects the cozy thought within the general doctrine. He says somewhere in Scripture that He does not grow tired. It was not for actual rest that God had used the word when He rested on the seventh day after six days of creation. Rather, it was a figure of completion, even a figure of a future rest. Now mankind looks hard at easy work; they do not want to taste this free sweetness or even rest. Their iron hearts through their minds make iron thoughts, raging thoughts against all grace.

Satan plots all things wickedly, whereby he disturbs the earth by means of his underlings; his dark hands work the threads unseen. He cannot act with his rage alone, nor can he be an obvious guest among his acquired sons, the children of sin. His wiles must yet be made against the will of man, as he sits still beneath the will of man. And so Satan lends himself as an invisible guide from the spirit air above, where the spirit creatures float. Among these is Baal, who can, it is said, fetch his form from the shape of man, or else, within his scope, the lesser shapes of toads, and in either form he had hovered over Canaan to make himself well-known. And there was Belial, lord of pride and lust, and other lords with him. Belial's sway made his name corrupt when people called him bad names, as he would eat the poor. He also sits in governments to make their feastings good and at the tables of poverty to make their morsels good. There is Moloch, who is smeared with blood, and who in every age takes babies from their life and makes people eager to have their babies dead. The trick is the same: let custom, not the weeping heart, be the heart. And there are more: Dagon, Ammit, Eligos, Furfur, Ziz, and many others, demons who are busy with their meddling.

All mankind tries, and there is no heart without a wound. All hide parts of themselves within a shady grove, behind a bower, even as Adam hid and patched his nakedness with leaves. A hand within the heart reaches for the mind; it thinks of itself as a sculptor and the soul as clay, and it shapes the soul in its way. One is too quickly made to know oneself and all one's parts, while the defending ramparts and the many shields know not that one is oddly made.

Wisdom is not for wretchedness or unpleasant restraint but for the good intent of life. She is on the lookout for humanity, to help them in all their goings-on, telling how one will reap what one has sown; that a snare lies wide-mouthed for the perverse, to eat him up; that a drunkard is emptied out with all his fillings; that sloth, slow and frightened of the forecast, quickly gets his poverty. There are more, and at every turn there is wisdom or folly for the taking. Wisdom has her hope included in the Hebrew law; nonetheless, the Law for Israel was not one of grace and could not sustain itself on much mercy. From its height, a rigorous perfection, the Law took itself to punish.

Now Israel, roaming about in the wilderness under the bondage of law, never had, even by slow gradations, insight into force of the Law, even when the Law repeatedly made scenes of death. In one instance, the people complained of the manna, having little regard to honor the miraculous provision that fell from heaven each day. They only saw their misery through the blindness of their mood. And they requested something else. A myriad of quails was blown into the ungrateful camp by means of a miraculous and perhaps mercurial gust. The next day, however, the Law interceded with antipathy and a plague, and many died.

In another instance, the Law carried that same passion, this time against Miriam, Moses' sister, who had spoken with begrudging imputation against Moses because he had married a Cushite woman with whom Miriam was displeased. When she had grumbled against Moses, God appeared in a pillar of cloud. He had her words considered sin and her estimation proved fiction. The Law judged Miriam with instant leprosy to correct the demand for justice. Miriam was covered, all white by the disease. A bad winter had fallen on her face. But Moses interceded for her, and God—provoked and bound, as it were, by the Law—reached mercy only after seven days, when she was taken back clean into the camp.

One may not yet see the spirit of a dove in the God of Israel, especially when one impatiently frames the Law around God's heart and calls Him strict. The impatient will cut reason short, and hope. Except one's vision is prolonged and broad, one will only see around the rim of one's own self, and that is very much a station in a ditch.

It is hard to argue with the Law when one wants to make a case for gentleness, and the reason for the Law has already been presented. However, the meek spirit of a dove stirs itself, and its aspect rises slowly with the rise of Israel—and through them, the birth of the Seed and the redemption for mankind, which includes the satisfaction and abolishment of the Law of Moses.

At this time in history, God had set Himself at His task to give a land to the traveling Israelites. The hope was for a land of rest and overflow, a new day, the rising of a pleasant sun; yet the people were tepid in God's heat and not riveted for land. After much traversing through the wilderness, the Israelites finally, wearily, came to the Promised Land. Twelve spies were sent out to check ahead. They did not return with the same hope as God, their strength impaired by fear. Their report claimed that this was indeed a land of milk and honey but that the inhabitants of the land were of the lineage of the giants, the Nephilim. In this discomfort, the spies made their disappointing case, in regret of the greatness of their foes—and perhaps in envy of the remarkable overflow and produce of the soil, a single stalk of grapes was carried by two men. Only Joshua and Caleb, of all the spies, had a good report, in spite of what they saw, and courageously confessed that they nonetheless would be able to take the land.

When the rest of the Israelites heard that there were Nephilim there, they lent their hearts to fear. Indeed, the sons of Anak, descendants of the angel-human hybrids, had wrought themselves upon the land. God was dissatisfied with the bad report of the spies and the lack of vigor in the people. He set out against them, not smiling, and planned to save only Moses—and from his loins produce a springtide, a new stream of people who would have a bolder intent than this placid and fearful cohort. But Moses intervened in this season of disappointment and asked God for mercy. God approved, but in compromise Moses had to wait out the people's hesitation, to recover forty years later when that generation had grown out by death and the young had grown up into a sturdier folk. Of the original batch, only Joshua and Caleb survived to enter the land.

Meanwhile, the Hebrew law, meant for blessing, made misery instead and left its loads all over the place. Korah and his friends one day took Moses for their subject and decided that Moses was lording his leadership over them. In this way they spurned God and Moses. When they were supposed to burn the fire offering with insensible cowering, they acted audaciously. Fire from God was in their way, and an earthquake of sorts, and the earth made there a mouth that gulped them all toward Sheol.

When the rest of the people saw the end result of the Law and its dreadful ambition, they grumbled against God. But the Law prevailed over grace and mercy and lashed out at them with a plague. Of the people, 14,700 died, and the insatiate Law would have gone further, had not Moses and Aaron come up with an offering to God that had strength enough in opposition. Some were saved, but the grief was not; and many went down the dusky paths of the midnight pit.

For many years, therefore, Israel traveled in circles again, waiting out the death of a generation. Sin and the colluding Law caused death and graves and murmurs all along. In spite of this God was yet good to them: the clothes and even sandals of this tribe, who wandered years and years, were kept supernaturally fresh and new in spite of the meanings of the wildness of the sands, and the treading, and the wind which ought to have ripped against their gear.

When God made covenants or laws, the advantage or enthusiasm was for the partners, not for Himself. And when the blessings and the curses were seen as a pair on an equal and rigid scale, God meant for man to be on the side of the blessings. He is not a cursing God, and when the trickster Balak, the king of Moab, endeavored to buy a curse against Israel, God withstood him. Now Balak despised this traveling tribe, which rumor had acknowledged as being conquering and victorious. And Israel, with all their overflow, were no longer at a distance. In fear, Balak wished to buy a curse from Balaam, a selfish prophet who had a peculiar power to effectively curse. It is unclear from which station the prophet had his power: he was outside of the supernatural domain of the covenant with Israel, in which there is a presumptive allowance of such transcendental forces, yet had a direct awareness of the God of Israel. Also he had no apparent condescension into what could justly be called sorcery. At any rate, his reputation was established, and the king of Moab sent messengers to Balaam to convey the anxious petition.

"A tribe came out of Egypt, and look, they are covering the whole land by their number; in fact, they are moving up to conquer me. So please come over and curse this people that I may be able to survive them and drive them off."

Balaam told the messengers to spend the night, and he would seek the word of the Lord in regards to the crisis. God answered Balaam and said, "Who are these people with you?"

Balaam returned, "They are messengers from the king of Moab, who is requesting that I curse the people who came out of Egypt."

And God said, "Don't go with them, and don't curse the people because they are blessed."

Upon hearing the refusal, the king of Moab again sent messengers, more distinguished leaders this time, so that the presentation might insinuate respect, and the urgency of the plea. And they told Balaam, "Please come and curse those people for us. We beg you; see the king will give you anything you ask."

Fidelity lasts as long as advantage, and Balaam suppressed or ignored the singular command God had given earlier, in his elevation of the ready prospect of money. He told the messengers again to stay the night as he would seek the word of the Lord, somehow hoping, in this duplicity to wait God out.

The manner of God here was somewhat perplexing, and there came from God the muted and dry answer, "You may go with the men then, but only say the words that I give you."

Still God was angry at Balaam and sent an angel to strike him. When Balaam came on his donkey, oblivious of God's intent, the angel stood in his way. Two opposing walls in a cliff were favored by the angel to have his insult, because the donkey and its master had to pass through there. But God was good and allowed the donkey to see the invisible being and the pending doom. The infamous donkey had sense enough to move as close to the side of the wall as it could. However, this scraped the irritated prophet's leg. With that friction in the prophet's mind, he lashed out with scorn and indignity and whipped the poor donkey sore. Suddenly the donkey had the facility of speech—God had opened its mouth—and the donkey said to him, "Have I ever done this sort of thing before? Why are you hitting me then?"

The prophet's eyes were opened and he saw the assaulting angel with his flaming sword. A fearful sensation ran through the prophet, and he conceded, in corresponding behavior, to prophecy a blessing on the Israelites instead. In this way the intended curse turned into a blessing and the hope of the king of Moab turned into despair.

Chapter 8

─────────────────── ❧✖❧ ───────────────────

Israel eventually proceeded to take the promised land, but it was only after they pressed in—the result of many wars—through faith that stirred the hand of God and through sin that rankled the Law of Moses. The native inhabitants, their enemy, had the sword of their armies often blunted and restrained to loss by God. Other times, the armies of Israel groveled back in defeat on account of the fatigue of their faith.

In between the Law and love, God had placed His mercy, and from time to time He had called judges to help Him and the people out. Though settled, the land was a precarious and capricious environment, and there was no single king or queen who could lead or unify the nation against the combative odds of their despising neighbors.

Othniel was the first judge, followed by Ehud—a left-handed man who had his sword hidden on his right thigh, so that when he was searched in clearance to the chamber of an evil king, he could come up close and kill. And there was Deborah, another judge, who had a tree named after her—the palm tree of Deborah—under which she sat to do her office. Indeed, she fetched prophetically a good word for Barak, son of Abinoam, when she summoned him to endure against a particular enemy.

The legacy of Barak is forever tainted by his shrinking behavior. As leader of the army of Israel, he ought to have kept the severity of his office and manly independence; but these virtues expired by the false guidance of fear. Barak was not sure of this defiance, nor of the hand of God, against the enemy and against Sisera, the commander of the foes. His faith was depreciated, and he insisted on going to war only if the protective presence of Deborah went with him to the battlefront. God and Deborah were annoyed by this lack of courage. To Barak's dishonor came another prophecy: seeing that Barak had not heart enough to conquer alone, his legend would share its honors with a woman who would kill Sisera by means of a tent-peg while he slept.

And indeed, during the victorious battle, Sisera, the commander of the enemy, had gone to the tent of a woman for a few hours of repose and sleep. Whether Sisera was too accustomed to safety or trust is unknown, but he fell asleep in the tent of the woman with comfortable indifference. The woman, being aware of the war, had hid her murderous intent with social propriety and an ingratiating manner. Sisera was exposed by the vulnerability of sleep, and she took a tent-peg and pierced his head.

There was Gideon, another judge and champion of God and Israel, who had measured himself in weakness, even when God appeared to him with a staff in hand. The commission from God was for Gideon to take down Baal, and on the same place make a daring sacrifice. Gideon forced his own obedience and tried his courage by doing the deed at night.

Gideon's and Israel's enemy at that juncture were the Midians. Now the Midians were a tormenting sort of people. Their raids into feeble Israel were spurred by the sport of it and by the arrogance of known superiority. Israel was unable to defend itself, and at this stage in history they were used to the bitter taste of subservience. For this reason, Gideon was afraid; and he carefully examined whether to provoke his antagonist, because no doubt they would retaliate. Gideon, in his anxiety, asked God for a sign, that it could encourage the willingness of his mind. God was fine to do the test: to change a fleece to dewy first and then the fleece to dry. The sign was a sufficient agent for Gideon, and he became powerfully kindled. In time, he rescued Israel from the hands of the Midians.

Years went on, and time and time again the Israelites made entrance for doubt, and with doubt made occasion for idolatry and sin. The lessons of history were unable to assume themselves as teacher, and frequent generations, in consequence, were struck by the adversity of the Law and the enthusiasm of their enemies.

God came to their rescue again and again, and in one such instance, He called Samson to help out. It happened that an angel appeared to Manoah's wife when she was working silently in the field. The intruding angel talked of hope and announced that the barren wife would be with child—a son who would be strong, who would be Samson. Manoah, the husband, when he heard this tale, wished that he had also been at the field, that he could determine the promise for himself through the benefit of sight. The angel, temperate, in the form of a man, again appeared in the field, this time while Manoah was there. The angel spoke fraternally with him of the promised son. The daring—or polite—Manoah inquired as to the name of the angel. But the angel was of his own name most reverent; it was not something to be taught. Yet perhaps the angel revealed it anyway, saying the name in the hiding thereof, that it was "Wonderful." Manoah made an altar, and the angel ascended in a flame through the fire of the rock.

In time, Samson broke through the barrenness of his mother, as he was meant by God to break the oppressive yoke of the Philistines, who had, like the Midians before, ruled and riled the disabled Israelites. Samson was a strange order of a man, a Nazarene whose method was physical strength when the Spirit alighted on him. There was no other muse for him except that false muse that assailed his great strength and moved him and sank him in the end: he was more glad for women than for life. At length he gave his divine calling a second flight; his first flight was to give his heart away to his wife, a Philistine. Herein was his guilt and weakness: his eyes gave away his heart, not the other way around.

Samson was to be married. In the cause of tradition and a polished wedding ceremony, he took thirty companions, Philistines, who would shadow him and cheer him on during the feasts. In the spirit of festiveness, Samson told his companions a riddle about a dead lion with honey in its corpse, which went like this: "Out of the devourer came something to eat, and out of the inedible came something sweet."

Disregarding the honor of self-discovery, the thirty men took their hopes to Samson's wife, to win the secret through a threat. His wife brought the matter to Samson and vexed him to tell the riddle to her as proof of his love. He told her the answer to the riddle, and she in turn, without fidelity, told the thirty companions. The grinning companions told the answer of the riddle to Samson, who accepted the answer with the gradual understanding that it was obtained through underhanded means.

Being furious, he went to Ashkelon. There was much sundering and chaos as he killed thirty Philistines and looted them. His wife soon afterward was given to Samson's best friend. On account of this, Samson's anger burned even worse, and in this bad temper, he took three hundred sorry little foxes, bound them tail-to-tail with a torch between, and let them flee in consternation through the fields of grain. The offended Philistines, in retribution, burnt Samson's former wife. Out of this came more anger on the part of Samson, and he came down to them in wrath and for a great slaughter. The ready Philistines had gathered three thousand men in opposition and stood outside the cave where Samson was waiting. Samson let himself be bound by them, but when he saw a timely moment, he ripped the ropes as one would flax, and with substantial strength and a donkey's jawbone, he swung at them and wasted them.

He would judge and help Israel in this way for twenty years, giving them relief from the frightened Philistines, who had reasonably and timidly acquiesced to the incomprehensible strength of Samson.

He judged in this way until he found Delilah. Now the Philistines came cowardly to Delilah, in private, to discover the secret of his strength. The unfaithful and greedy Delilah had her eyes on eleven pieces of silver, her reward if she could entice Samson and persuade him to give up his source. She pressed him and played as if there were between his secret and his love a prejudice. In time he told her what made him excel: that his strength was in his hair, which had never been cut.

One night a man came to their home. Delilah had lulled Samson to sleep, and the man cut off Samson's seven locks of hair. Then the Philistines came upon him, and as he had no longer strength, they beat him and removed his eyes. The Philistines were in glee, and when they later held a feast for their god Dagon, they called for blind Samson to make sport for them. His hair had meanwhile grown, and the Philistines were ignorant of the return of his strength. In a scene of sport and mockery, Samson was placed and chained to pillars. He lamented to God to end it all and to help him try out one last act against the Philistines. Now Samson's arms were around the pillars, and he cracked them. The feast ended with their deaths, and his vengeance ended with his own life.

Chapter 9

An ebb and flow of victory and defeat continued in the generations of the Israelites, and the blessing of the covenant was often retracted because of their sin. In one such generation, a drought was facilitated by the curse of the Law, and Elimelech and Naomi left the land in sight of hope toward the land of Moab. They went there to see what they could do. The land was less withered there, more green and fruitful.

While in Moab, the couple had two sons, who grew up and added to the family by taking two Moabites as wives. Naomi's husband died in time there in Moab, as well as her two sons. One of the daughters-in-law did not take to the new domestic dynamics and left Naomi for the Moabites. But Ruth, the other daughter-in-law, laid aside the bond of her native blood for her loyalty to Naomi.

The drought was over, and Naomi, when she heard of it, moved back to Israel with Ruth. It was the time for the barley harvest in Israel, and Ruth would glean with a good hand behind the reapers. This was the custom for the poor, to reap after the reapers. In dishonor she walked and worked in bended form in the fields; hunger might have been easier, but Ruth thought of Naomi, and her honor was her cause.

One day, when Ruth least expected change—or patronage—a man named Boaz came riding on his horse. He was the owner of the land, and a good man. His wealth and stature supported dignity instead of the easy conversion to pride. Boaz was kind toward Ruth on the field, and when Naomi heard of this, she revealed that Boaz was in fact a relative and could redeem Ruth, as it stood in the laws of their culture.

Naomi and Ruth decided on the best way to proceed; they did not want to flatter Boaz away or to intrude too hastily. Therefore Ruth, in this method and some days later, washed herself and added oil for shine and watched Boaz when he ate and drank. When merriness and sleep came to him, she moved up gently and lay at his feet on a stack of hay, because Boaz had gone to sleep on the hay. Boaz woke in the middle of the night and found the unfamiliar woman so reposed. She spoke to him, when he came to his senses, of herself and of him, the relative who could redeem her and cover her.

He said to her, "You don't need to lie at my feet anymore, because I'll redeem you. I'll also honor you in this, because I know that you could've given yourself to a younger man but have spared yourself for me. There's one other relative who is above me in the line of the law of redemption, but in the morning he should answer whether he should be your hope or not. Meanwhile, stay until the morning and lie down as might a sister."

The next day Boaz went to the gate. This was the custom for making deals, because the elders of the town would sit in this way, in wisdom and for memory, to mark thus any new contracts. The elders at the gate heard the story of Ruth and Naomi and of first rights. The first relative answered and gave up his right. Boaz took Ruth as wife in consequence, and there was joy and more joy when she gave birth to a son, Obed, who was the father of Jesse. And Jesse was the father of David and other men too within this lineage, by which at length God produced the Seed.

Chapter 10

— ❧ ✖ ☙ —

The Seed was not yet, and it was still the time of the judges. Next came Samuel, who grew up in the house of Eli, the priest of God. Destiny can have strange turns and crooked paths, and the great Samuel started off lonely. His mother had, in her wisdom and honor, given Samuel first to God and then to herself. As for her love, she went once a year to see her little boy, who was now reared with Eli in the temple. Each year she made a little tunic for him, which he in constant love would wear. Much love was left for him each visit, but not enough to fill his heart all year long. And what she could not do enough, God did when He took Samuel for Himself and loved him.

At this time in history, there were very dark days in Israel, and the word of the Lord came infrequently. The material world and the habits of the natural mind had curtained off the voice of God. Still, the mercy of God was available for help. One night Samuel heard God speak with a voice that called his name. Now the boy was unready for this, and he thought that Eli, the priest, had called him. Twice he ran to Eli to see what he wanted. At length, Eli made the correct assumption and told the boy that he might hear from God, that he should answer next time, saying, "Speak, Lord, for your servant is listening."

Samuel returned to his bed; he lay awake in anxious curiosity and said to the voice that called again, "Speak, for your servant is listening."

God called Samuel to be a prophet, and for his first task he had to tell Eli of God's judgment on his house—this because Eli had not restricted his own two sons, who were in spiteful variance with the holy things of God. They had designed their roles for money and for lust. Eli himself also sat much outside the expected ambition of God inasmuch as he went lazily about in the daily rituals of his order. He was old and feeble, in the winter of his years, and he had resigned his fervor to God to the influence of his perceived season.

Meanwhile, much of Israel was also caught up in this cold and doleful repose and was likened to Eli, whose eyes had gone dim. There was something more splendid in Samuel, something of a lovely spirit that could likewise make all his actions lovely, when he as a determined wing against the winter winds would fly, and a whole nation would turn back toward their God.

Israel's turning was a slow turn, their hardness not so quickly soft. And when at first they fought against the Philistines, they were perplexed as to why they had lost. In one such battle and defeat, there was the saddened exclamation about the ark of God, which was taken as spoil by the Philistines.

With the ark as loot, the Philistines looked down on Israel with smirking condescension. However, the operation of their faces soon changed to a more miserable aspect. It came about that the ark was placed triumphant in the house of Dagon, the god of the Philistines, but when morning came, it told of something strange. In the morning, Dagon was on his face; an angel had pushed the statue down. The baffled Philistines in determined conscience pulled Dagon back up erect. They did their best not to think the worst of it—until the next morning when Dagon was on his face again. This time the angel was more instructive in his zeal and had broken the statue's head and arms with impatient fury and had strewn it before the ark of God.

Now the ark was in the region of the Ashdodites, who became more sure that this object was an antagonist with which they could not happily deal. God's hand, not heart, had troubled them because of the ark. A strain of moaning followed from the Ashdodites, and the leaders of the Philistines acquiesced to the complaints and eventually took the ark to the land of Gad. Their purpose had examined a better place for it, yet there was moaning again, this time from the people of Gad, because God had smitten them with tumors. The local diviners were called in to see whether they could find an answer to the anomaly or come up with a pardon and to learn if there was any way to make an excuse to this God and His ark and get it away from Philistine by whatever means.

The diviners came up with a solution: there should be molded five golden tumors, cast exact, and five golden mice for the achievement of their peace—or for penance in case it was the custom of the angered God. The golden objects of mediation were placed on a wagon along with the ark, and two milk cows were harnessed up front. The milk cows were picked deliberately, as a test, because the diviner here had a sense of chance versus God. Therefore they had build the test to force the hand of the one or the other: if the cart went one way, it would be by chance; if it went the other, it would be by God.

It happened that the milk cows (cows that had just had their calves and would always yearn toward them) pulled away toward Beth-shemesh, and so the people took it to be God's hand. The cows went lowing all along the road as if actuated against their will. An angel was walking upfront, leading them and the ark on to Israel.

In this way, the ark returned to Israel, to Beth-shemesh. The local people of the town had more curiosity than wisdom when they saw the ark. They looked inside and meddled with the holy ark. God's wrath broke out, and nothing soothed the people when they saw their dead. Fifty thousand people died, the expense for their easy looking. The remaining people were uncertain what to do, how to work with God.

This morbid train of stretching death was because of holiness. In absolute terms, God is at variance with sin and will not for love's sake be at variance with Himself. Love and holiness are both bright in God, yet none will outshine the other, nor to the other give compromise. Holiness has to do with a thundering self, and within this indomitable vivacity are no other currents, no strange crossings, no ebbs or fleeting flows, no shadows that in nooks might grow. It is not the faint warbling of a chatty stream that needs to toss itself at angles at every curve or rock. Rather, it is the cavernous roar of a great water. Its only border is itself.

Holiness and mercy are in apparent paradox. There is an innate concept of God's sovereignty—that He can do as He likes—interwoven in mankind's perception of His acts. Herein too is an incomprehensive paradox: God is at once all sovereign yet limited. As far as the doctrine of God's sovereignty, there is much to be said. There is a silent belief in providence: the idea that God is pressed to assist when called upon and to answer for any or every calamity that may occur. More specifically, it is a belief that reserves no place for evil, nor any responsibility on the part of a person, nor the doings of the Devil. Intuitively one is aware of God's omnipotence, and therefore falsely and clumsily supposes God's hand and His entrance in whatever good or bad occurs in mankind's varied occasions.

Others are more convinced of fate, but one should rather have God over fate. The latter is not to be trusted in optimism, as fate, being blind, does not look out for our good. One should rather lean toward something with a heart. To what then can one credit all the capricious growths in life? At times a person's own fancies give him or her their trouble, the consequences of sin; at times others willfully interpose themselves offensively in another's steady path; and at other times, Satan introduces himself objectively—he has a whole index of unclean spirits at his service and uses them imaginatively in his war with mankind.

There are many crags within the soul, and in many a crag a demon sits. For this reason, God has sent the Seed to reverse all of this antagonism, to bring the people to a secret place of shelter. Even though God has the capacity to govern all of His estate according to omnipotence, He does not stray a little from His will, and He is as a judge who follows his own laws. See then God's committed diligence when He gave independence to humanity. He was unable to retract this action when He saw them going to the furthest end in sin, choosing to make their will against His will. God is not concentrated in the harsh hurricane for destruction. Indeed, even the earth groans also for the manifestation of the sons of God, so that it may be set free by them from the primordial curse.

The thought of omnipotence takes a natural turn to the concept of God's omniscience—His all-knowingness, His foresight. Did God conspire with omniscience to let Eve sin? Integrity and risk have offices in His heart, and He cannot bend His laws for love. Truth is the strength that takes the hallelujahs to the throne. The praise of a natural mind will pause along its drift; it stops at every flaky cloud, its strength only in its throw, and there is no angel's fan to waft the heavy words up high. In fact, His heart is as easy as the dove. One may see a fault in meekness, but there is also a corresponding torrent that beats within His heart. The flesh is not wide enough for all His loving flood. Humanity needs another gate, a greater gate by which a sweet mouth—as a suckling on the abundant breast—may drink from His pleasure. One may find it hard to divide His goodness and severity, being perplexed at life and at the perceived lazy providence. God is limited by man. Yet humanity is not left hopeless; they need not sigh at God or look around for Fate. God has made a way.

The worldly mind, in doubt, tries at life with private skill, with effort. Other minds that treat self-effort as too high for them, find comfort in the group; they hide among the rest for safety, like a group of spotted fish that have their hope in numbers, hoping that bad Fate will take the one out yonder.

But faith has a better hope, and meantime, Israel hoped under the Hebrew law for a salvation that was brewing but had not yet appeared. When Samuel was old and unable to go further, the Israelites eventually asked for a king. They should be as the other nations, they all said, to have for themselves a monarchy, that they should in this way have their order and their strength.

During this time, there was a man called Saul. He was after the pattern of a king, and for every pleasant feature within man, he excelled even more. He was in his face handsome and exquisite, and from his shoulders up, he was taller than the rest. It happened that he was on the lookout for his father's donkeys, which had gotten lost as they had mindlessly grazed. Saul pursued them, and when he could not find them, he said he should return, because—besides the worry for the donkeys—his father would worry about his son.

Saul's servant, who was with him in the search, wanted to try one more time, to go to the seer Samuel and inquire as to the donkeys. Saul agreed but wondered what to give the prophet in case there was a fee for his far-sight. The servant had a shekel, which they thought would suffice. Saul and his servant went up looking for Samuel's house, and on a slope along the way was a group of young women. The seer was at the end of the hill, they said to Saul.

On seeing Saul, Samuel told him where the donkeys were and that God had eyed him to be king. Saul was baffled and did not carelessly accept. He wanted to know how this could be, as his place was in the humbleness of the apparent lesser tribe of Benjamin. Yet Samuel anointed Saul, and Saul set it privately in his heart.

Soon after, Samuel called a general summons of all Israel to choose a king by the casting of a lot. The lot fell on Saul. Young Saul was embarrassed by the honor, and he was led on by this inhibiting emotion to hide behind some baggage. The lot had first fallen on the tribe of Benjamin, then on the Matrite family, and then upon Saul. There was a big crowd present, and when the lot fell on Saul, they looked enthusiastically for him—but he was hiding.

Chance may be bad, but risk is good. In life, many people throw the dice and dance upon the numbers. A chance is taken, and knowledge is weaved therein. Many see this world detached from the order of a giving God; therefore they have no calm lake on which to steer their careering boat. Risk itself is not the wobbly invention that fear can imagine. For that matter, risk is the style of God, part of the brave spirit within Him. And in all His beauties, His daring shines as bright as might a knight against a foe, who his own size does not reckon, but his heart. He is as a sower who, with none left but the last and only seed, leaves it in the ground and waits in hope around it.

Something of this nature of risk must have been a feature in the hand of God when He made the earth and all the angels and mankind, and when He spread the vector of light and, therefore, the possibility of dark. He could not within His own daring stay idle. He took a chance on man; better the risk of loss than the loss of risk. Therefore, He created in a manner that He Himself could not deny; even His omniscience could not His hope outgrow.

Meanwhile Israel peddled with the casting of a lot, in this case with the aid of God, and the lot was on Saul, who was hiding still and knew not what else to do. Then God spoke and said, "Saul is over there, hiding behind the baggage."

The people came and took Saul and insisted on proclaiming him king. In spite of this meek beginning in Saul, his heart and the range of its actions reached the rank of valiancy, and he was a sharp blade to his enemies. In this way, he freed Israel from the dominion of the Philistines. His blade and the thrust of his courage were praised by the esteem of his people. The zeal of praise is not concerned about pride, and when Saul was unable to support the adulation with the strength of his humility, he was assimilated into an unpleasant and hard state of mind. He made a monument of himself that had the haughty eye of stone. And other things he did as well, such as when he laid presumption at the foot of God, disregarding protocol, and refused to wait for Samuel in an offering to God.

Saul eventually discovered that God was displeased with him. He tried to correct things with words, but meanwhile the Spirit of the Lord had departed from him. In the absence of this protection, an evil spirit visited him and tormented him. It is unclear what the demon breathed into Saul's soul, what exact vial of poison it had chosen from its dark apothecary. At any event, a glum and conflicted mood ensued. On one such occasion, when Saul was in a fit, his servant suggested that music might help, that a man skilled in the harp should be asked to help the king become less inflamed. Saul agreed, and young David, who was a musician and a shepherd, was called to give Saul his good songs. Now whenever David played the harp, the demon would flee, roaming dry places until it could set itself up again against Saul.

During this time of Saul's personal conflict, war was still going on, and the Philistines and Israel had many campaigns, and the lines of the troops went back and forth for wrath and war. David's brothers were at the battlefront, and David's father had an anxious wish for news of his sons. David was at home at this time, having a respite from the moods of Saul, and David's father sent him out to inquire of his older brothers.

David was sent off with food: an ephah of roasted grain and ten loaves for his brothers, and ten cuts of cheese for the commander of the thousand, for goodwill. So the young David went up and walked around the outskirts of the camp, seeing how it fared in war, and then deeper in, where he found his three brothers. Just then, something bad called out into the air from the lines of the Philistines: the mocking voice of Goliath, a hybrid Nephilim, who was loud and obscene and who made dreadful forecasts to the eyes of the beholders. The soldiers of Israel were afraid and remained quiet in the safety of their line. David was curious and asked his brother what was going on and what would happen to Goliath. But his brother got angry and said to David, "Why are you here at the camp, anyway? You've come to snoop and to see the battle. And what of the few sheep you've left at home?" David was abashed and replied that he was only asking. But his brother was not in the mood to talk.

When Goliath came out again to mock Israel, David muttered that he himself would take on the giant. It was heard within the camp that David had said this—and also in the court of Saul. Saul, therefore, summoned David to see whether he could be of use, and he fitted him with his own armor. Concerned, Saul advised David that he might not make out as well as he wished.

David's frame and spirit could not fit into Saul's armor; it was too heavy. David felt he was best in tenderness and without all these arms; his heart had this enough. A humble sling and five little rocks would rise against the boasts of Goliath. History has replayed this battle over and over: the strange Goliath and the shepherd youth opposing. Mankind's invented sight sees the legends fight, and those who witness it say how good it is that the least can overcome the greatest. One's heart cheers David on and sustains him with a boosting shout.

As for David and the actual event, his bravery was not alone, because he knew that the scales were set and that the weight of words from the opposing giant weighed less than the present weight of God. And so it happened, a moral deed and a mortal rock went well in speed into Goliath's head, and afterward came the lesser art, when David cut the giant's head off and heaved it upward in victory.

As a result of this, there was an extension of favor to David, and he was thus promoted to the army and elevated with laudation to sit, surprised, at the king's table. Saul's son Jonathan had his heart knitted to David, and he amazingly disregarded his own ambition in favor of the shepherd boy who would be king. The people were of the same conclusion and furnished the embarrassed ears of David with songs of praise, singing of David's ten thousands—and of Saul's thousands. The offensive song caused the disadvantage of a burning jealousy in Saul. Unfortunately, Saul admitted the emotion to his immediate mind and stirred up a baneful storm within himself. The scales tilted, and Saul's once safe affection for David became unequal in comparison to the weight of his fuming about. Saul threw himself against the self-made storm and worked himself against the wind and against God. Saul's insecurity sustained the tempest, and he rummaged about until it grew out an evil thing. He devised a scheme and thought on the angry thing so much that he eventually approved of it and defined it nicely within his wish for vengeance. He became its instrument, and it promoted him to its own hand.

Soon after, when David was once again playing the harp for Saul, the mulling emotion and hot blood against David spouted out, and Saul threw his spear at David to pin him to the wall. But neither the provoking youth nor Saul's agitation were tamed by this. There was a brief tumult in the room; David jumped to the side with the alacrity of speed and fled from the presence of the sulking Saul. From then on, Saul sought unsparingly to have David dead. Saul's mind was full of ideas and in all degrees looked around for a clever way to kill him. Something surfaced at last when Saul discovered that his own daughter was in love with David.

The mad Saul believed she would be a snare to him through her influence, making David either relaxed in capitulated love or exasperated by the spirit of his wife. He believed that David would be unable to single out his spirit from the mix and would falter when he faced again the fields of the Philistines. He gave his daughter to David, yet the preferred ruin never came about as Saul had conceived. Instead, Saul's daughter Michal, now David's wife, had her heart set on fidelity, and once, when Saul's men came to get David, she stuffed the bed and placed a quilt of goat's hair for a disguise and then let David through the window to escape. She did the best she could to play for time, and when Saul's men finally broke through the door, she acted well and said she'd had to acquiesce to David because he had said to her, "Why should I hurt you?"

Meanwhile, David was on edge and fleeing though the lands. At length he came reluctantly to the land of Gath. David learned that his own legend had spread ubiquitously into this foreign land and that the fierce eye of the king of Gath wished to have sight of him. David was soon spotted. Therefore, David was afraid, and he indulged himself like a madman, by which antics he might have a possible escape. He broke out fiercely into a wild act, dipping his body into every mad thought that was considered commonly mad—saliva from his mouth dripped to catch the eyes of those askance, and other things he did to preclude the perception of sanity. He grabbed a stone and scribbled upon the walls as if he had found himself a writer, stuporous yet prolific in some sort of glee. The king of Gath had no great time beholding this and said that he needed no madman in his courts.

Back at Saul's compound, the circumstances became dire. The lines of Philistines were more daring. Ordinarily, Samuel, the seer, would have given advice and foresight as to victory, but Samuel had died, and Saul was no longer taught by the Lord. Without this instructive voice, fear spoke to Saul. Discouraged by the foreboding scenes of war, Saul decided to obtain another guidance—this by means of pretense, taking on the disguise of a common man—and seek by trickery the fidelity of a spirit-medium.

Saul was aware of a woman at Endor who could raise or summon spirits from the dead. When he came to the woman, she did not recognize him, because he had substituted his royal apparel with a costume. He requested her to invoke Samuel. The woman did her ritual and somehow shaped Samuel out from the mists of the spirit-world, from Sheol. Whether her acts were previously satisfied through pretense, or whether the lazy spirits' risings were sometimes exaggerated by her performance is unknown; yet here, in this instance, the woman was surprised at the actual appearance of Samuel from the dead. She cried out in fright. She saw Samuel provoked, and she saw at the same time Saul without his cover.

The ghostly Samuel said to Saul, "Why did you bring me up from the ground? And why do you call me from my rest unnecessary? You can't do this, because first, God has given you His disapproving sigh and also has given David what He can't give to you. Tomorrow you'll die, and Israel will be outside your hands into another."

When Saul heard this, he was as a man stretched out, his body and his thoughts stifled and supine. The medium, who was less perplexed, bent over to comfort Saul and was better to him than his own heart. She served him food, her fattened calf and unleavened cakes, which he ate serenely.

Saul died in battle the next day, yet many of the remaining people of the house of Saul refused to sheath their swords and anxious hate and continued to make war against David and his followers. In time Saul's descendants and support got weaker, and David at length could assert himself. He eventually was crowned king, and all the tribes were satisfied.

Chapter 11

————————— ⊰ ❈ ⊱ —————————

Absalom, David's son, had the same peculiar fault as the rest of mankind. If worth or self-value is not perfected in the heart, the mind will not exempt anything in its quest for this fulfillment. And Absalom said to himself, "I will be king."

At this time in history, David was still king; so Absalom came up with a scheme to usurp the throne. He was aware that the population was at times like sheep, going this way and that, and in any direction that might be prodded by the measures of a gentle stick. He presumed, therefore, to tamper with subtleties that ought to move the spastic herd. He launched out with pleasantries up front—a golden smile coursing as helm, the rudder of need and pride active from behind.

The plan consisted of a show of affection and command. Absalom rose early in the mornings and stood near the gate. With him were a chariot and fifty men to give a hint of marvel. And whenever a person passed through to seek the counsel of the king, Absalom would call this person to his chariot and look downward and talk kindly as if he understood. In this way, he intimated that he could give more lenity and justice than David could. The coddled person was then persuaded by the simple trick.

In time the unwholesome scheme paid off, and Absalom flattered his way into the populace. After Absalom had wrested away enough support, he went after his father, king David. David suddenly discovered the long-grown conspiracy and its matching danger, and he saw in the situation that he did not have enough men on his side to resist. He fled, with Absalom in pursuit.

Absalom's hair was very long. During the chase, Absalom rode high on his donkey, and when he passed beneath a tree, his hair got caught in the branches. He hung there, not knowing what to do because he was alone. He could not get the branch to relax, nor could he through frustration free his entangled hair. At the same time, Joab arrived—David's commander—who speared the hanging Absalom three times in the heart. Joab had refused to obey the command that David had given his soldiers—to be gentle with Absalom if he was caught.

Consequently, David returned to take his seat as king, and he had for many years a more definite and stable kingship.

Years later there was trouble again when another rebel, another son, stood up with private enthusiasm and said, "I will be king." This man and disloyal son was Adonijah. He was inspired by the fatigue of the king, because David was old. One day Adonijah summoned the sons of the king and some other noble people to a gathering, a dinner of sorts. The sons of David had gotten wind of Adonijah's intention, and they came that they might have favor in case his plan to usurp the throne worked out.

Meanwhile, David was on his bed, spending time in dreams because he was very old. His nights were fuller than his days. His wife Bathsheba roused him awake and said to him, "Have you heard about Adonijah, how he has quit his own heart and you, O King? He has made himself a lord and king outwardly. Think of Solomon, your son and mine, and let him be in your place esteemed. Hurry then, before Adonijah can waste your heir."

On her words, David stirred strenuously from his bed. He called for Solomon immediately and had him there on his bed made king. Zadok the priest was also called, and Nathan the prophet, to anoint Solomon as king. And they were all in a hurry and told Solomon that he should on this occasion go outside and ride on David's mule, and a trumpet should blow ahead of him, giving merit to the new and actual king. All this was done, and even David, from his bed, bowed as he could to Solomon.

Meanwhile, Adonijah was still busy with his feast of assumption. He was becoming more sure of his seat because of the modesty of his guests. His curious study of their eyes saw their hidden fear and their willing partiality. Yet while he was glancing over them, a noise was heard coming from the city. Trembling, he heard the austere report of Solomon's new height and of his own below. When the other sons of David heard this, they neatly excused themselves and fled, wishing to escape the coming trouble. In this way Solomon was established king.

One night God came to Solomon in a dream and asked him, "What can I do for you? Ask anything."

Solomon asked for wisdom and understanding so that he could rule God's people properly. What was the least was most, and God added to his request honor, peace, and much wealth, the inevitable and natural gain from wisdom, understanding, and knowledge.

Solomon, owing to such panoramic prosperity and favor, became stronger than all the other kings around, and his name and grandeur are forever mentioned in superlative terms. Even the great queen of Sheba came to see what was going on, and what she heard somewhat in rumor was extolled by her when she arrived, because she exclaimed that the rumor had left out half of the abundance.

One day, two women came to Solomon. Their tears were affecting. It had happened that both had given birth around the same time, and both were happy until one of the babies died soon after. One of the women said to Solomon, "The babies were exchanged at night. When the other found her baby dead, she placed the dead one at my side and took the live one to her side."

But the other woman said, "No, it's not so. I didn't take the baby. Rather, she's in grief for her child and now wishes to have my son as hers."

Solomon thought about it, and he ordered his guard to go and cut the live baby into two halves, to let each woman have a half. The actual mother exclaimed that the guard should stop, that she would rather have the baby whole and alive and would give it up to the other one instead. The false mother said, "Go ahead. It is fairer to have half a baby than to have none at all." And Solomon halted the guard and gave the baby to his mother.

During Solomon's reign, Israel prospered, and everywhere and in everything, wealth and peace had a supernatural felicity of growth. Solomon indulged himself in all the wealth and power and admitted no exceptions in his accumulation. He took for himself seven hundred wives and—besides them and unexhausted—three hundred additional concubines. Many of the women were foreigners, because he had a preferred inclination toward them. In time they were too divers for him, and they wrested him away from his commitment to God.

Sin sometimes sprouts slowly to death, as death is slower than the deeds thereof; it slowly stirs toward the poisoned fruit. In time, a disappointed God spoke to Solomon and told him that the kingdom would expire after he died—that He had for David's sake postponed the ripping away of the kingdom for the next and worse-off king.

The next king after Solomon was Jeroboam, who was raised up for the coming apprehension. One day Jeroboam was traveling on the road, and the prophet Ahijah met him. Ahijah, in a prophetic figure, took hold of his own cloak and tore it into twelve strips. This was the figurative measure of a pending Israel, torn as an intractable consequence of Solomon's sin: he had lost his heart and worshiped Ashtoreth, the goddess of the Sidonians, and Chemosh, the god of Moab, and Milcom, the god of the sons of Ammon.

Later on, another man of God came to Jeroboam. This man of God prophesied to Jeroboam that he would one day burn the priests of the high places. Perhaps Jeroboam felt that the forecast came from a self-inspired man and that his words were scraped together by invention, the homeless arrow of a prophetic want-to-be. The uncongenial Jeroboam reached out his hand to grab the prophetic man, but as he did this, his hand froze, like a branch that drought had dried up. Jeroboam's arm meant more to him than pride, and he came to his senses and appealed to the man of God to renew his arm to life. The man of God prayed, and God immediately restored Jeroboam's arm.

Being impressed, Jeroboam invited the man to come with him, to sit across from him in friendship and with food. The man of God declined, saying that God had commanded him to go straight home and not turn one way or the other, nor eat with anyone, nor sidelong pass when he went back to his home. And so the man of God went on his way.

Around this time there was another prophet, an older man who was retired, and on account of his age and mood, he idled around at home. He heard about the young man of God and the miracle that had occurred, and it aroused the old prophet wondrously, because he had used to attend to the things of God. As for the old prophet, ease had withered him, and he had neglected the sanctity of his office within his heart. So when he heard of the man of God, a mass of curiosity and envy provoked him to energy. The old prophet had his son saddle up his donkey, and off he went in a hurry to intercept the young man of God.

When the old prophet found the man of God, he talked to him approvingly and admitted that he too was a prophet of the Lord and wished for the man to acquiesce from his speed and come with him to eat. But the man of God said that he could not, that God had told him to go directly home. The situation was for the old prophet too much of a delightful and titillating thing because he had faded in himself for so long, and he did not want to pass this up. Therefore he lied to the man of God and said that an angel had come to him and told him to say that the man of God should veer and pass through the old man's house to eat. The grand story of the angel laid caution—and God's actually command—to a distant rest, and the man of God veered off and sat to eat. As they sat across from each other, the amused old prophet suddenly felt again the true word of God, and he spun himself around in confidence. His first fabrication had served as a mild tonic for his complacent life, but the actual word of God that now appeared made him feel fertile and properly useful.

The old prophet was suddenly adherent to obedience, and he said to the young man of God that he would die because he had come to sit and eat. At first the old man's word was supported within him with glee, but afterward the subsiding emotion and aftermath gave way to uneasiness and misgiving. He knew he was to blame for the coming death, having solved his envy with a fatal trick.

At any rate, the words were enough for the young man of God, and he left and was back on his road. As he traveled, a lion jumped him from the side and killed him. The lion, for some reason, sat beside the corpse, not eating it. Back in his home, the old prophet heard of the corpse and the lion sitting by it, and he saddled his donkey and went to see, or undo, the troubled temper of his guilt. When the old prophet arrived, the patient lion still maintained the corpse that lay beside it. The prophet took the body and did one thing decent when he buried him in a good grave. He told his sons that one day when he came to his own end, he must be laid there at the same grave also.

Chapter 12

Many years followed, and in them the undaunted fortitude of the Law ruled and tossed the bungling and disqualified Israelites. There is a stem for every fruit, and at this weary juncture in history, another king, called Ahab, rose up and diverted his people into worse idolatrous vegetation. Also from this figurative unclean trunk, there appeared a lonely fruit, hanging as though foreign from the common roots and stricken branches: it was the good prophet Elijah, who was thus set up against king Ahab.

The antagonism was marked when Elijah predicted a terrible drought in Israel. During the drought, God sent Elijah to a widow in Zarephath. When Elijah came to the city, the widow was there gathering sticks.

"Bring me a little bit of water and some bread," he asked of her.

"This is the situation," she returned. "I'm making a rare meal, my last, and I'm getting my last sticks together for the last bit of food. I'm making it for me and my son, and then when we're done eating, we'll lie down and die. But nonetheless, I'll make the meal for you instead."

In this way the widow surpassed herself and placed her kindness before lament. Elijah answered her that the bowl of flour and her jar of oil would, by itself—or rather by God's hand—not

❈ 77 ❈

empty out. It happened that the famine could not move the ample bowl and jar, as its contents supernaturally multiplied.

As for the rest of Israel, the source of their hope was in what they saw around them in the flesh, the sweetness of what was known, their corporeal milieu that was the heart of them, their manifesting god. The spirit of Elijah had a different pulse; it beat in spite of and adverse to the dark vector of the common life, like an eagle flying strangely and divergently against an opposing wind. And the spirit of Elijah pressed hard against the spirits of the age, even against death, raising the widow's son from the dead. Israel, with their doubts, saw more use in the dust of the earth. They abandoned the sky for the comfort of the land.

The sun sets and the moon comes up, and one is duped by this familiar work as if it plays out independently, as if it always has and always will. Yet all this movement of the natural and all its machinations are subject to the tick of a superior chime and higher kingdoms that wield their mighty strokes. The spirit of Elijah was a harbinger of the high air above, confronting all spirits around about him. And if the clay, the natural, sings a lowly song, there comes an outside voice who makes his song superior and clarion.

Now king Ahab, who had subsided into the clay, had his silent soul enticed by the spirit of his wife, Jezebel. It is true that when a person refuses the good waters of the wise, he or she will be disposed, as though in stupor, to have the drink elsewhere, from the brackish waters of a lesser well. From that water, the notorious Jezebel expressively drank: she was a conduit of the Baals, through which she made her scene and influence across all of Israel.

Whatever good was left in the people was reduced by this couple, and evil and trouble came in abundance in consequence. The unfortunate Israelites took to the Baals and were unable to differentiate between their former God and their happy idol. The denseness of the dark and hovering air of Baal was too much for the placid people to refuse. And if any had doubts of the new god, the stammering mobs of devotees and the continuous, triumphant cries of the prophets of Baal would soon sweep the indifferent person heedlessly into the new cultural norm.

As though to perfect the error, king Ahab killed the prophets of the Lord—yet some were saved, hiding in a rock. It was a big mess, and figuratively, springtime was abandoned for a wretched spiritual winter. So when God's people were meant to move the sap up their branches in strong virility, they were lulled by pale Ahab into sleep. Ahab himself lived and slept in a high steeple made of stone. Within the royal steeple stood Jezebel as well, awake, beautified, and vain, looking from her window spot, and her eunuchs also were there, softly tending her hard look.

One day Elijah came to Ahab and said to him, "How are we going to do this? Let us test this Baal and see whether you'll still bend to Baal when he rises not to you."

Ahab returned, "Is it you, Elijah, troublemaker of Israel? What do you want? Very well, I'll set up the Baals against your prayer."

The defiant test involved four hundred and fifty prophets of Baal who were staged around their altar on one side. The condition of the test was for each faction to prepare an offering, and when the sacrifice was ready, the true god would move to answer by unleashing a supernatural flame. Therefore the prophets of Baal were around their altar, but however instructively they prayed, the godly flame fell not for their sakes. Later on, when time took their first hopes away, they became desperate and used the strength of their anxiety, along with whips to flagellate themselves and much blood, that they might provoke the silent Baal to their aid. But it appeared that Baal was unable to respond to the frenzied pleas, so the prophets of Baal sank and waited for Elijah's turn.

Elijah raised the stakes. When he had the ox laid on the altar, he added pitchers full of water, poured on top with confident provocation, so that he could more definitively show the coming fire. Then Elijah prayed, not wailing. There was no need for a loud voice calling far off into desolation; his God was nearby. And

God sent fire onto the sacrifice, and it licked up everything, even the water, which could not force the fire out.

The people of Israel, who were watching the contest, saw the fire in awe. They rose up as one, unable to endure the Baals any longer. They acted quickly on Elijah's word when he told them to take the prophets of Baal and do away with them.

Jezebel heard of the deaths of the prophets of Baal. Her anger argued for revenge, and to Elijah she sent a message of the measure of her potent will: to have him dead by the next day.

Surprisingly, the amazing miracle that had just occurred failed to assist Elijah's faith and bravery, and his recent dare seemed like a short-lived wind that had blown itself away. He heard Jezebel's warning with acquiescing trepidation and ran for his life—all the way to the area of Beersheba—and sat under a juniper tree. He was weary and slack, and he asked God ironically for death. Perhaps self-pity was to his pain an unsuspecting foe, and from its manifesting lull, it brought into the apparent calm no balm of hope. In that moment, Elijah lay down to sleep underneath the tree, to welcome in sleep his requested death. Yet he could not put death in this way into his life, and an angel appeared to this end, poking the sleeping Elijah in the side to wake him up. The angel gave Elijah a jug of water and bread cakes baked on hot stones.

The food and water recommended some happiness to Elijah, though he refused, being miserable, to learn anything beyond ease from it. He ate and fell inflexibly back to sleep. The watching angel was not much into all this sad sleep, and he poked Elijah again, and again offered food and drink to him. The angel added that Elijah should eat and drink because of a long road ahead. Elijah rose and ate a second time and admitted to a better future, recognizing that he had marked himself too early for death.

Whatever was drawn from the angelic food, it sustained Elijah for a subsequent famine of forty days, during which he ran all the way, without sleep, to Horeb, the mountain of God. Elijah's sprint was equivalent to divine alacrity, a supernatural speed by which he dashed passed by bemused farmers, galloping horses, and bewildered donkeys. At length he arrived at some cave, where God saw him sit, somewhat unconvinced. God asked him, "What are you doing here? Go up instead on the mountain."

Whether it was placid obedience or enthusiasm to hear God speak is not known, but Elijah climbed up to the top. There Elijah waited on a rock for God to make Himself known. A loud wind passed by, one that in its magnitude split the rocks around. Elijah stood up and checked it out, but God was not within the wind. An earthquake followed, without lenity, yet God was not therein. And afterward was there no anticipated calm, because a fire broke out—though it also went out, burning only for itself—but God did not burn within. Soon after, as Elijah watched, a gentle blowing came, and Elijah wrapped his cloak around his face, because he knew God was inside the benevolence of the breeze.

On the mountain, God told Elijah to return and interrupt the wicked king Ahab—and to take Jehu and anoint him as the new king. God also told Elijah He would retire him and substitute him with someone called Elisha.

It came about soon after that Elijah went down and found Elisha, who was plowing in the field. Elijah walked up from behind and threw his mantle on the stunned Elisha. In this way, Elisha instantly received his call. Surprisingly, Elisha accepted the call and sudden change with relative ease, and he followed Elijah.

An eagle sweeps along on the winds of change, but the hen in placid wonder of her nest is content to ignore the moods of the sky. Her sight is on the little worms around her, having no farther sight or plight to fly off into vaster straights above. The hen is too soothed to bother, yet there are birds that scorn the ground-bird's wings and are better trying out upon a branch. Now these midway birds cannot greet the sky as might the eagle; because of the branches, they cannot see that high. Many people admit to a sense of something ascetic, something supernatural. Some have, in spite of this awareness, sunk their wings and poked only at the passing by of things amidst the dustiness of earth. Some others, more inspired, have their invented hope in clever spells to prevail against Fate.

A residual is left within the recesses of the soul, a sense that it can force its print by thought upon natural life. And it is indeed true that the soul is not utterly discharged without a shade of spirit or a residue of potency, perhaps the remains or echo of the breath that breathed in Adam. After the fall, and in the scarcity of spirit, the soul concocts still a supernatural that can seed the clouds above—though with a clumsiness of hand, from an estimated point of view—whereby the soul affects the destiny of the life of clay. The fallen soul, because of the forces flowing from the heart, thinks herself quite smart when she boils her cauldron in this way, making impregnation with her rising smoke. The soul gives off her perfume, and this aroma is applied naturally to the treatment of destiny. The natural mind should be alert that the odors contending within its leaves stay fresh, avoiding the rottenness within the branches and the bark; otherwise, bad life may grow agreeably and fastidiously on its former green. But God provides a better way, that the soul may lean its face toward true life, being born again through the implanting of an actual and new spirit, wherefrom all the flowers and all the fruit ripen up within the fine fragrance of His summer.

Now there was a fruitful vineyard in the time of Elijah, and king Ahab had in his rottenness envied the vineyard for himself. The vineyard belonged to Naboth the Jezreelite. At first Ahab could subtract the weight of a bad conscience from his proposed trade, because he offered to Naboth the price of the field for the price it was worth. But Ahab was soon sullen, because Naboth refused, saying that he could not sell it to the king because the field was an inheritance. Ahab returned to his palace and was not in need of anyone, because he was looking to the wall on his bed and brooding miserably.

His wife, Jezebel, found him there, waxed, and told him to feel better in that she had hand enough to get the field for him. Naboth was unaware of the proliferation of the scheme, because

Jezebel had quietly written letters to the elders and the nobles of the city for each to play a part—and to two worthless men who would be used to accuse good Naboth of something bad.

A pleasant dinner was arranged with all the trappings of a lure, and Naboth was invited to sit at the head of the table with the nobles all around. Naboth anticipated in the face of the cordial scene, naturally, that some honor would be smilingly granted to him. The mildness of Naboth was unsuitable for what happened next. The two worthless men suddenly stirred and lied and said that Naboth was, among this circle, guilty and foul and that he had behaved badly toward the king, having cursed both God and king. Though Naboth denied the accusations with all his heart, he could not deny it otherwise by any act, because the false words festered and smoldered in the surrounding crowd, who stoned him to death in a spontaneous and gruesome impulse.

Naboth's death was disdained or ignored by Ahab—except that his mood improved. He rose up with the prerogative emotion reserved for a child, or the childish, and he went out to take possession of the field with Jezebel nearby, urging him on and gleaming. There was a certain swelling of Ahab's face as he took the field, but the greedy widening lost its effect when Elijah suddenly showed up at the field as well. And when Ahab saw Elijah, he said, "Have you found me, oh my enemy?"

Elijah answered, "I've found you. And I carry with me the word of God that will bring you down for all the evil you have been up to. Though you've lived your life aloof, you'll die low, because dogs will lick your blood for your low honor—and dogs will eat your wife for her lack of honor."

The words frightened Ahab, and the telescoping vision of his future pulled him to some of his senses. He became despondent for a while, and within that despondency something of humbleness laid. Much judgment was meant to be achieved against Ahab for all his sin, but it came about otherwise than the supposed wrath, because God said soon after to Elijah, "See now what king Ahab has done; he is not as bold-faced as before. Therefore, I won't draw after him soon with the promised stroke; My love can hold off some until the time of his descendants."

It came about that Ahab and Jezebel lived many years still, because judgment was moderated by Ahab's stint in humbleness; but meanwhile their enemies around them stirred up even more. There was war, and Ahab, king of Israel, and Jehoshaphat, king of Judah, drew up together in the field against their antagonist, the king of Aram. Being nervous for his own sake, old Ahab said to Jehoshaphat, "Why don't you dress yourself familiar, with your royal robe, while I'll dress in disguise."

Now the soldiers of Aram were on the lookout for Ahab, as his death on the battlefield would provide to them an unequal advantage. Poor Jehoshaphat, meanwhile, in royal garb, felt the arrows rain on him. He acknowledged the precarious colors of his outstanding robes and gave in to haste, and he gave too the picture of a great escape from many men speeding after him, their spears and their horses' heads upright in the sweet sense of a victorious hunt. Meanwhile, Ahab had the advantage of his disguise and had veered into the mix of the battle.

From the camp of Aram, one warrior, battered by the chaos of the clash, felt that he at least could shoot some arrows into the sky that they might land where they may. One arrow was for judgment bound, and it hit Ahab in his side. Ahab died, wounded, and was buried. The last of life bled out into the pool of Samaria in the square where the harlots bathed. There were dogs living in the square, and they licked the blood off the ground.

After Ahab's death, Jehu entered into the historic scene and was made king after him. Jehu had set it in his course to take revenge on the house of Ahab, and in this assumption he went to a place called Jezreel, where Jezebel was staying. She had often from her high tower downward perused, and with her look had made up the best of haughtiness. When Jehu and his soldiers arrived below, they saw the bad glare from her eyes.

"Who is with me?" Jehu called up.

Three officials in the tower gave sight of themselves through the window of the tower, and with nodding heads they showed their agreeable intent. Jehu called to them to throw her down. Her death was swift in the tumble. Jehu gave word to bury her for the sake of decency, but word returned to him that this would be difficult, as only parts of her body remained because the dogs that lingered there had eaten it.

Chapter 13

— ❧ ✖ ❧ —

It was a rough time, and poverty and war instigated a great famine, especially in Samaria where an army had besieged it round about. A donkey's head, for food, was sold for an exorbitant eighty shekels of silver.

One day the besieged king of Israel walked around and beheld in dismay the weary state of the people. While he was walking near a defensive wall, a shrieking woman called out to him. He asked her, "What's the matter with you?"

There was something awful in the sound of her voice as she related this: "O King, while my love was always present for my son, my hunger overreached, and I boiled my son and ate him. But I had done this in agreement with another woman so that we could last longer in this place of craving, to give each of our children in turn for food. And I was steady with the plan when we ate my son the day before, but now when her turn comes, she hides her son from me."

The violence of the account propelled the king into shock and an active temper. He tore his own robes and had the preferable idea that this was somehow the work of Elisha, his opposing prophet, who must have prevented the prosperity of the land and all God's strength. Therefore the king exclaimed, "For sure, I'm going to get this Elisha, and today I'll have his head."

The king and his men came to Elisha's door, but before the men could strike out, Elisha said, "By tomorrow at this time, a measure of flour will go for a mere shekel."

Now the officer on whom the king was leaning said, "What nonsense! How is it possible for this to happen?" And the king and his men left, wondering.

The origin of the miraculous deflation in price and instant prosperity was hidden in the least likely source. Four lepers, on the same day, were passively sitting outside the besieged city, forcefully excused because of their infectious illness. In that moment they reflected on their condition and said to each other that they might just as well do something extraordinary. Why be timid prior to impending death from hunger?

"Let's go over to the camp of the army of the Arameans that has besieged the city and walk in boldly. If they kill us, then it is all the same, and if they are gentle, then we'll be more than we are right now and live a little longer."

Their hunger promoted their plan to sufficient bravery, and they set out. Around twilight they came over the hill, near enough to face the camp, struggling to walk and muttering to each other to say their last words, if they could. The twilight hour or the barren hills added to the noise of the lepers, and the minds of the Aramean soldiers, conditioned for war and perhaps fear, heard the distinct approach of an army. And when the soldiers saw in each other an example of their apprehension, they worked each other up into a sense of an impending dread. This effusion happened too fast for anyone to give a second thought as to the sound, and the soldiers tore out of their tents and in haste left all they had to leave, taking nothing but their fear and dust, and ghosts of armies that seemed to storm them from the hill.

At length the four lepers came wandering in and were dumbfounded at the sight of the empty camp. Their hunger thought first of food, and they ate as much as they could of the abandoned spoil. Greed surfaced next, and the lepers took silver and buried it for themselves just outside the camp. At last a sense of morality or conscience confirmed itself on their minds, and they said to each other, "It's not right that we should be so full in this time of famine. Let's go and share the good before the time is up."

They returned to the gate of Samaria and related in a good mood the recalled scene of the abandoned camp of the enemy. The gatekeeper heard the vital news and sent and woke the king, because it was night already. The king had no easy greeting at the tale and said it was a trap, saying, "The Arameans left the camp because they think we'll be—in our astonishment and hunger—bereft of reason. And then they can be against us easily when we wander carelessly into their camp."

Nonetheless the king's curiosity divorced his caution from anticipated danger, and he wanted to proof the story one way or another. A small group was sent out to check the camp. These returned, saying to the king, "The circumstance is no longer supposed, because it's exactly as the lepers said."

Sleep was lost that night and the next day, because the people of the city were as a swarm that went out and savagely looted the camp of the enemy. In that day, poverty capitulated to overflow and envy to greed, and Elisha's words came true after all.

The shame of the nation and their misery grew in time, and apart from a few kings who were good, most kings in each succession were vacant toward God and ignorant of the covenant in which their blessings lay. These evil kings, in spite of their efforts to moderate success without God and outside the covenant, introduced more evil into Israel; and the people themselves, with this apparent permission, had no eager footing for the Lord and viewed their degeneration and their misery with a sort of laxity. At length, Israel had broken the covenant so sufficiently that the demands of the Law terminated in judgment. A great dispersion followed, a great deportation into the oppressive dominion of the land of Babylon. It was a terrible turn for a nation, a destruction and unimaginable collision with the comparative and once stately reign and overflow of the kingdom of Solomon.

Chapter 14

⊰ ❈ ⊱

Many years followed—and even generations—with Israel bound under the yoke of a foreign land. Yet God had put His heart in a remnant of people in whom the memory of Israel was not entirely degraded.

Nehemiah, an exile, had this dream more substantial than others, as God had stirred it in him, and he felt this thought cleave his mind so that he could not find himself without it. Eventually his constrained ambition reached the features of his face, quite literally, because one day when he was serving before King Artaxerxes, who had conquered Israel, his private mood was evident. Nehemiah was the server of the wine before the king, and the king asked him concerning the busy aspect of his face. Nehemiah felt he was in trouble, because it was against propriety to come before the king with the lax effort of a distracted face. One had to please the king. Then Nehemiah related to the king how he thought about forgotten and scattered Israel and desired to rebuild the walls of Jerusalem, that it was this yearning he had attended to instead of the king.

Somehow the king did not mind the little offense and was pleased with Nehemiah. The king granted him extended days off from his royal service to go and do the thing that was on his heart. The generous king gave Nehemiah letters of approval and also a letter to Asaph, the keeper of the king's forest, for the provision of timber for the beams of the gates. The forecast was good, and Nehemiah went out eagerly and impatiently.

Yet Satan was against Israel, and he stirred up a couple of men, Sanballat the Horonite and Tobiah the Ammonite, to be against Nehemiah. The news of the rebuilding of the walls was fatal to compassion and productive of hate, and these two men became terribly roused and burned with anger against the project. They could not to themselves justify why their hatred had become distinct within; hate foregoes the sources of its instigation, at any rate.

The first scene these two fiends made was to cross the margins of Nehemiah's courage in the hope that they could diffuse his happy strength. Mocking words and ridicule would do the work of their cruel intent. The objective was discouragement, and their method was humor mixed with scorn, because they thought there was power in a slight that was somewhat droll. In the face of accusatory comedy, one feels always on a lesser leg, not knowing what do to at first, because the venom lies or stirs in the aftertaste. In this way, Tobiah and Sanballat loved their hate. If a fox were to run on the new wall, it would crumble down, they said to everyone, making sport and rumor.

Nonetheless, Nehemiah and his people were sustained by God through all of this, and they kept on working. Disguise is a first instinct in man, but when Tobiah and Sanballat and their gang saw Nehemiah's resilience, their masks were taken off with combative zeal, and with their faces bare, their hearts rose into their eyes. They conspired openly how to make their point with actual force. Nehemiah heard of this and set up guards, which were needful around the clock that their work might not be reduced to the convenience of the enemy. By necessity and in this way, the work was diverted, that in their one hand was a weapon and in the other the tended burden of the labor.

The general mood of enthusiasm among the builders and their families increased their strength and peaceful commingling—but not for long, because the workers had provided of their own income to the project, and some had entered into debt. They needed to mortgage their houses for food and borrow for the payment of the king's tax, and some had to sell their daughters into bondage and their sons for slaves.

Nehemiah heard the honest grumbling and gathered a great assembly, including the rulers and nobles who owned the people on account of their debts. Nehemiah gave a speech and made a fierce case, pregnant with ebullience, fairness, and brotherhood. The landlords and lenders were moved, and they devotedly capitulated to help their compatriots with financial absolution.

Meanwhile Sanballat and Tobiah were not done with their striving. Therefore they came up next with something rude. They did not blush at this, nor could they, as conscience was dead and unable to paint that pure color.

Evil goes after conscience first, and the voice of mercy has no longer voice within the roar of malice that bellows that there is no God, that you might as well get in life what you can get, since there is nothing else besides. The smiles of their teeth are sharp as a knife and flash as a spear. The devious mind scoffs at good and is glad for it in that it may be a prey, in that it may be an undistinguished member of a flock of nervous sheep, a soft species open to a wolfish bite.

Sanballat and Tobiah sent to Nehemiah a private note that they should congenially meet in the plain of Ono. The intent hidden in the pleasant invitation was not concealed from Nehemiah; he saw that they wished to harm him on the plain.

"I can't come," Nehemiah sent back. "I'll lose time at work if I spend time with you."

Pretense was dropped when Nehemiah did not acknowledge them, and Sanballat and Tobiah increased their intention to blatant opposition. They sent another message, saying that they should therefore by compulsion meet, else they would go to the king and complain that Nehemiah and the Jews were in secret pledging for revolt, that the ambitious Nehemiah planned to make himself a rebel and something of a king.

Despite the possible consequence of the accusation, Nehemiah kept on working, giving them little regard. The two rivals, exasperated, came up what they thought was indeed a stupendous plan: they would send a spy within the walls, one who might pass as innocent and therefore clandestine, one who could have eyes for them and, by his seeming good intent, lure Nehemiah to light up something of comradery. Then, when the spy was a sufficient muse and had grown cleverly familiar, he would come to Nehemiah with a fear, warning him to desert the work and flee.

The spy would be Shemaiah, who, according to the scheme, ingratiated himself into Nehemiah's inner circle and one day said to him, "Let us hurry and flee and hide in the temple, because I've heard some things of death, that a plan is fixed, and for tonight. For tonight the plan is for your death."

There was also a prophetess, Noadiah, who had attended artfully to the same scheme, giving so-called words to Nehemiah, as if by them he might know his time and know that he was not invincible.

Somehow the solid, or perhaps stubborn, Nehemiah resisted the crafty advice and the duplicitous prophecy, and he never flinched. In this way, the walls came marvelously up—and this against the backdrop of all the awful noises of the dark, the screeching and the barking of the creatures of the night.

Jerusalem was therefore established, and though the city and the walls did not shine with the glitter of luxury, it sustained a wonderful sight of pride in the people. The vacant city needed a populace, which was solved by the peculiar mandate of a lot: lots were cast and one out of ten of the scattered exiles were summoned to return and live in Jerusalem.

Chapter 15

—— ⊰❋⊱ ——

In the days of king Ahasuerus, Israel was still largely ruined and spread out, waxed insecure in other dominions and foreign lands, there to feel lost or, if they had resilience, to make as much as they could of life. King Ahasuerus, who reigned from India to Ethiopia, felt it pleasant to breathe out in one shot a good sigh of his royal satisfaction and contentment for a hundred and eighty days. This he did by the example of a splendid feast that was carried out to this stupendous length—all for the delight, or dismay, of his princes and his dignitaries. The king was to be acknowledged for all his splendor, and indeed his stature had the semblance of all overflow. Hence he chose this extended display to give all a sense of his wealth.

After the passing of a hundred and eighty days, the king added seven more days of feasting to be held in the court of the palace garden. Guests from the least to the greatest were invited to enjoy the astonishing overflow. There were hangings of fine white and violet linen on cords of purple, silver rings, marble columns, and couches of gold and silver on a mosaic pavement of porphyry, marble, mother-of-pearl, and other precious stones.

At the end of the seven days—when the king was at last more near to merriment on account of the wine and had softened into ideas of pride—his thoughts were light on propriety. He called forth Queen Vashti for display, because she was beautiful. But

Queen Vashti was annoyed at the invitation to the extent that she refused to appear before the king and the unfair eyes of the king's noblemen. The king thought her behavior spiteful, and he was not content with only anger. He inquired from his nobles what would be the best thing to do. The nobles advised him to solve the issue, otherwise it might grow in its fever when it left the court by rumor. It would be, they said, a pervasive example for the women of the empire who would get a scent of it and act likewise and would for no reason rise contemptuously against their husbands.

The advice was taken with concurring acknowledgment by the king, and he easily gave consent for an edict: Queen Vashti did not make it as the queen anymore and must be, red-faced, deferred to the outside of the royal court.

This happened in this days of Esther, who was by the ties of her blood a Jew and, of course, an exile. She had all the good effects of beauty, not only in her face and pose, but also in the finer arrangements of her soul. Now King Ahasuerus regarded the unoccupied seat of Queen Vashti and ordered his eunuch, Hegai, to go at large within his kingdom and gather virgins who might be drawn into his harem. They were to be taken care of in the royal courts and blossomed-up by cosmetics, whereby they could be purged, so that at length the one who had the most could take the seat of queen.

In the seventh year of the king's reign—after the season of Esther's beautification —she was brought to meet Ahasuerus face-to-face. He liked her enough, and during a merry feast, she was made queen. She suppressed the pride of station, and she was silent all along about her race, keeping it secret—along with the identity of her uncle, Mordecai, who had indulged in her success with a fatherly doting and apprehension.

Now this Mordecai was a particular man; his heart beat with a stubborn pulse, and he had no thought that clung haphazard on the waysides of his mind. He was himself a storm and smote with innate conviction all lesser thoughts away. He had told Esther to be quiet about herself, and meanwhile he had walked loudly outside the palace gate and stomped up and down each day that he might hear how well she was getting along.

One day as Mordecai was imposing himself around the gate, he overheard a covert dispute, a lethal plan by two fellows, Bigthan and Teresh, who were angry at the king. The mind of Mordecai, with its oven and felicity of heat, could not pass the conspiracy to the side indifferent, and he told Esther of the plot. She in turn told the king of the slaying that was in the air and of Mordecai who so lived for the king. For his own cause, the king got hold of Bigthan and Teresh and made them not come back.

Meanwhile, the king had promoted Haman over all his kingdom. This Haman elevated himself in his own mind and believed everything that fitted his pride. All the other lords and people were soft toward him, bowing whenever he passed for his recognition and honor. But Mordecai refused and was at his fullest whenever Haman would stride by. Mordecai would not bend at Haman's appellation but stood deliberately as if of wood. After observing successive disdain on the part of Mordecai, Haman was filled with rage. He laid his anger in a strong disguise, acting as if he did not need to condescend. Yet secretly he retreated far into his gloom and imagined all sorts of wicked speculations to soothe the slight against his state. From then on, he decided to retaliate with reproach against the welfare of all Jews, because he knew Mordecai was a Jew.

At some point in time, Haman came to the king and set up a good face for his bad plan. He told the king how the Jews were, among the peoples of the kingdom, like something set aside, that they did not contribute much, that they withheld themselves from the traditions of the kingdom, living with spite and prejudice against the ordinances of the empire. Haman went on to advise the king that it was perhaps in the best interest of the kingdom to place them out of sight, to have a chance of recovery and make the kingdom strong by making all the Jews within his scope extinct.

It is unclear what followed exactly in the narrow mind of the aloof king, except that he must not have been strong in this instance, as strength is seen in what is just. And strengthless, the king made an edict to wipe out all Jews by death. The murder would commence and diffuse on the thirteenth day of the twelfth month, when all the provinces were to tend to the execution of the edict, condemning and slaughtering the entire race.

The edict inevitably disturbed the repose of the now frightened Jews, and as the day of their death approached, there was a great outcry from them, a great wailing. Esther also had a faded gaze and wanted to speak up for her people. She would approach the king uncalled-for and would roam near his quarters; if he held out the scepter to her, she would live, and if not, then it would be otherwise. Meanwhile, Mordecai sent to Esther a message: she should not think that she had no fault in her. Her queenship and its gloss would not be enough to escape the fate of the edict, and besides, perhaps she had been advantaged by God and placed for such a time as this.

The Jews in Susa knew Esther planned to approach the king uninvited, and they fasted to God for her sake. The day came when she dared to go before the king, and she came up and stood before the royal quarters. The king saw her there waiting, and he extended the golden scepter, which meant at once that she should not die and that she might come up close. It must be hard to trust only in the mood of a man, but at any rate, all was well, and Esther was glad that her boldness had received favor. The king asked her whether there was a good thing he could do for her. Only if he could come rejoicing to her banquet, she returned, and Haman too—a banquet for the three of them.

Haman was high on this good news and marveled to his own wife and friends on how good he was, that even the queen invited him from among all others as a star. "Things would be even better," he moaned, "if only this Mordecai would not treat me with such posture."

His wife and friends had advice: "Make gallows and hang Mordecai on the poles."

The gallows were made for Mordecai's death, and a banquet was prepared for the king and Haman. It so happened on the night before the banquet, when the king would rather sleep but could not master it, that he came hard awake and called for the scribes to read him something of the history of his reign. The midnight scribe hurriedly grabbed a random scroll, anything that might render the wakeful mind of the king back to fatigue and sleep. The scribe read on and on and eventually came to the story of the conspiracy against the king, of the indiscretion of Bigthan and Teresh, and also of Mordecai, who had watched out for the king.

"Was this Mordecai ever considered for his good deed to me?" the king interrupted.

"No," the scribe said, "he was not acknowledged."

It must have been morning by then, and at that very moment of the reading, Haman came walking in for work. The king, seeing Haman, asked him what he should do for a hypothetical man who had used himself in a dapper way for the king.

The self-orbiting Haman thought the king was making a reference about him, and he said, "Such a man who is this great ought to be seated on the king's horse and led about in this circumstance through the city square, wearing the king's royal robe, and a noble prince ought to take the horse around, to lead this special man in a dazzling display."

The king thought it was well-expressed, and he asked the now thunderstruck Haman to mount Mordecai thus and to lead him round the town distinct.

Evening came, and Haman recovered himself from his humiliation. He went to the banquet and was in a better mood to eat; his day so far had been awful. All was swell within the festive mood and the effects of wine and food, till at length the king asked Esther what he could do for her, if she had any petition for his consideration. One has never waned so fast or become so less bright as Haman did when Esther stood and said from her heart that her people had been sold to death, that an enemy has contrived this plan that, for all its trouble, could not compensate the king. The king at that moment relinquished his ease and asked who could have such agency, who could this presume?

"It is this Haman!" she cried out.

The king did not know exactly what emotion to attach to the charge, and he got up to his garden, there to ponder and calibrate a notion. At length, when the king could endure himself, he returned to the banquet room, where he saw Haman fallen halfway on the couch where Esther was. This was because the frightened Haman had meanwhile pleaded to Esther for mercy, but he had, under the influence of the wine and his dread, stooped unbalanced on the couch and upon Esther.

"Would he even assault the queen?" the king exclaimed, as he entered the scene. As these words went out of the king, they covered Haman's face. A chamber servant, seeing felicity in the moment, revealed to the king concerning the gallows that Haman had made to hang Mordecai, who had spoken well on behalf of the king. Everything was too much of a boisterous stream within the king, and he ordered that Haman himself be hanged on it.

There was still the other thing to govern, the troubling edict to have the Jews all gone. Concerning an edict by the king, once sealed, it had a competence of its own and needed no other power. Therefore the king could not undermine his own edict. Yet by the advice of Mordecai, who was promoted to the king, another and quick plan was formed to rule over what could not be ruled away: that on the thirteenth day of the twelfth month, all Jews were permitted to be on their own incensed and to fight those who might draw against them for a kill; that they were allowed to work for the defense of their lives. In the space of time, the dark day arrived, and the Jews held fast to their survival. Many enemies were slain, and to this day there is a remembrance of the event, a custom set up as a vestige that is called the Days of Purim, after *pur* (the lot), which was once cast so low by Haman.

Chapter 16

— ❧ ✖ ❧ —

Imagine if there was a person who, with extraordinary intellect and wisdom, searched everything around him for the truth of life. Now Solomon had set out with his great mind to find the truth of mankind's lot through the wonder and meaning of it all, and *everything* meant both good and bad. Therefore, Solomon said to himself in the drafting of his search, "Come, now, and I'll test all this life with pleasure. Perhaps there is something in it. I'll give myself to every conceivable pleasure, in case the truth of life lies there."

In this way Solomon applied himself and permitted himself anything and everything. At length he delivered to himself his own intriguing report.

"I looked into pleasure to its extreme, under the method of wisdom, inasmuch as wisdom was my preserving guide, that I might not have my eyes on something too far off and find too late I could not move my tempted eyes away. Certainly there might have been unapparent bait, I thought, and for so able a master as pleasure, I needed to be careful not to be its slave. I put myself to a lustrous life and did not deny myself any pleasure that might be a pleasure for a man. In such a way, I enlarged my works, building houses for myself, making gardens and stupendous parks, making vineyards and an industry, water ponds for irrigation of the forests of my growing trees. I added male and female slaves and brought silver and gold into my collections, an overabundance as an overflowing stream, treasures from all the regions as none has had before. I made no excuse for frugalness; in art, I was full, singers hired for my pleasure and concubines for my bliss.

"Meanwhile, I watched all this as from above, as from a prudent and serious view. At last I saw that all this was like striving against a wind that blew with vacant hope; it was vanity. My spirit was down, yet I thought I should not pass my sadness by. Let me be mindful of vexation or some other madness. Let me parade past my strange thoughts for the sake of my inquiry. I wished to see if there was conviction or some truth in sadness or loss, a beauty in its hideous disease. Yet there was no winning thought nor feeling in this madness or melancholy; this station too was a paralytic vanity. Nonetheless, something was raised from all of this: wisdom exceeded folly as light exceeded darkness, and there was no enjoyment without God.

"I went on and pondered times and turns, whether these might be consulted for my cause, whether there was an advantage in the rising and the setting sun. Why should it so persist, beginning in the morning with wide announcing glaze and rushing back again to captive dusk? And of the wind, there seemed to be no end. Without a steering will, it was off toward the north, then swirling back toward the south, and it laid not still—for what? And what was this thing called *time*? A saw no channel to the past; when a thing was done, I held it only by its whisper. And what was future time? When it arrived, it was as if it were not new. The seasons did not ask me whether I was there; they came and went in their appointed days: a time to plant and a time to uproot what was planted, a time to throw stones and a time to gather stones, a time to search and a time to give up what was lost.

"Yet I saw eternity within the hearts of men, and I knew not why exactly. In the domain of the heart a wickedness exists, and in the place of righteousness an evil lives, a fox and not a fawn. In spite of all the good effects of man, they died as beasts and had no other eagerness; this too was vanity. Concerning this wickedness,

I saw mankind divided into oppressors and oppressed, that both had need for comfort, but no one took their tears. My journey took me to a certain man, whom I spotted in my search. He had no son or daughter, yet he pressed himself in a course for wealth. Indeed his eyes saw nothing else, saw only wealth, and this too was finally a grievous task.

"I shook all things in my grabbing reach. They quivered as undefended objects for my exultation or disdain. This was not some pointless roughness in my search but was to see if I could find the bottom of it all and so perhaps sustain my little hope with an idea that mankind's lot was more than what I saw. But time and thoughts fell far from what I had hoped; no new idea could thwart my futile thoughts. I might have wished, in time and in despair, to condemn all motions of man's life as spoiled from the root. Even so, I assuaged my downward thoughts with circumspection, an end point in my search: mankind is not so utterly fugitive, and sweetness has means at times without an intermixing bitterness; happiness has some worth.

"Yet from birth to death, an empty life and chasing steps run causeless with so much drive. What is the advantage then? Naked he is born, and naked he will die. Yet there is something fitting in that a man may eat and drink and enjoy his labor under which he toils during the few years of his life. Maybe even wisdom has no good augment, because a wise man, seeing more, is concerned therefore with grief, while the fool, who sees not much at all, is sustained in the gladness of his ignorance. In spite of this, I surmised that a wise man is at length the better man.

"I went back and forth in hope and movelessness, and in the end my wisdom, my philosophy, could not come to truth—even though I had reached with it beyond the reach of other men. I received my conclusion with stark discomfort, perceiving that I only understood my wide look in very narrow terms and that the days I had put to work had made my sincere wisdom give up, being taken over by the heavy-handed dominion of mystery. My search was in lower flight than that which flew above—except for one conclusion from it all, which was not defeated by the height: to fear God and keep His commandments."

Solomon's pessimistic conclusion, taken alone, will admit only expense. His view or discharge was the result of the natural mind, which does not have the scope, skill, or privilege of the spiritual mind. The latter's piercing intellect has no actual entrance to truth. The natural exists for itself, and in spite of its exertions, it cannot think beyond the proportions of the flesh. The eye of flesh sees only flesh and is hostile to the spirit, approaching it at a distance with connivance and distrust. But God does not leave humanity in this weakness, nor entirely ruined with the unbreakable force of flesh.

The work of Solomon has one finish—the same as Job's—that mankind needs something *other*, a redeemer who can with lovely truth reduce futile toil to hope and set the panic of humanity's mind to the reasons of His mind.

Solomon, nonetheless, came in his afterthought nearer to the secret than when he was in the discomfort of his circumspection. Solomon went on to write a splendid and romantic song, *The Song of Solomon*, wherein God's plan and mankind's truth were softened into the eloquence of a lover and his love. So God is, as Solomon said, the rose of Sharon, the lily of the valleys; and like a lily among the thorns, so is she, His bride, among the maidens.

Chapter 17

—— ❧ ✹ ❧ ——

Of this Groom, God had a good enough prologue, even when He used flawed men, prophets of old, who looked at the great day from far off. The prophet Isaiah was one of them and was not impaired in sight when he saw and spoke of a marvelous sign: a virgin shall be with a child and bear a son, and he will be called Immanuel, meaning "God with us."

When Isaiah made the strange prediction, the gaping Israelites were not assured. Yet Isaiah went on, satisfied to have his words as prey to the frowning brows of his audience.

"And the people who walk in darkness will see a great light; a child will be born to us, a son will be given to us; and the government will rest on His shoulders and His name will be called Wonderful Counselor, Mighty God, Eternal Father, Prince of Peace! There will be no end to His government, nor of peace. And this kingdom will establish and uphold justice and righteousness from then on and forevermore."

The thing was just too mystical for the people to understand, and they were unable to simplify it for the common contemplation of their natural minds. "Life," they said, "is always part of death. We don't understand this hope you talk about. We're tired and take tired life on, and if green life is found instead—sunshine for a fleeting life—then it's only the stray grace of a distant God. But don't talk too loud of hope, of miraculous salvation, of the promise made to Eve. We think life more void than not of happy plots."

Isaiah went on, declaring that God would swallow up death for all time and that, in time, the people would say of God, "This is our God for whom we have waited; let us be glad in His salvation."

The faithful Isaiah must have been perplexed at times at his own utterance. In one such divine vision, Isaiah saw the outlines of the Savior and saw Him marred, saw that He made with His own blood a sprinkling, saw that He was despised and forsaken by mankind, a man of sorrows and familiar with grief. Even more strange—and even paradoxical—Isaiah saw this Man, the Messiah, being smitten by God as in affliction, being pierced for the sins of all people, crushed and led passively like a lamb to a slaughter.

Now the people to whom Isaiah spoke had no pleasure in the mixing of these images, and they were opposed to the recognition that a savior could win in apparent defeat. Their own little hopes were stronger in the picture of a warrior king who could save them with muscle, who through his outward strength could make mankind swoon to faith and awe. They did not understand, nor did they wish to have their freedom free.

Isaiah revealed that God had first looked around into the hearts of man to find at least one who could be an instrument to deliver them. And God was astonished when He could not find even one with strength enough to save the others. Then God, for love, used His own arm to bring salvation to mankind. In this prophetic picture, God came down as a man, putting on righteousness like a breastplate and a helmet of salvation, garments of vengeance, and the wrapping of zeal like a mantle. As for the vengeance, it was not against the face of man; instead, wondrously, God rose with His blade and pierced Himself, becoming the substitute. Thereafter, for justice's sake, He took compulsory death and was not well in Sheol. There He had judgment and wrath to spare, and red-colored and single-handedly, He judged the sprawling demon spawns, taking away the keys that Satan had of death and Sheol.

Isaiah went on with His saving God and asked prophetically, as in the bliss of a vision, "Who is this One, majestic in His appearance, marching in the greatness of His strength?"

"It is I," says He, "who speaks in righteousness and is mighty to save."

"Why are Your clothes red, like one who has treaded the winepress and got splattered?"

"I have trodden the wine trough alone, and from the peoples there was no one with Me; I had looked and there was no one to help."

Meanwhile, God was not hushed regarding the redemption, and as He peered about to make more prophecy, He found Ezekiel, to whom He introduced Himself conspicuously. It happened while Ezekiel was by the river Chebar among the exiles that the heavens opened, and a great cloud, a striking wind, and a flashing fire appeared within the mix. Within the glow was another glow like that of metal in a flame, and deeper in, after the pattern of the human form, were four living beings. Perhaps they deserve some other name, but the senses here implores for sense in the beholding of these beings. Each had four faces and four wings. Their legs were straight, and their feet were like a calf's hoof, and they were inflamed as by a terrible holiness like burning bronze.

Ezekiel saw them kindle as he stared at them in a powerless gape. Their faces would his eyes overtake, because he did not know how to look at them. Each had the face of a man, the face of a lion on the right, the face of a bull on the left, and the face of an eagle so that each looked out thus with four faces. Their wings made them more exulted—a pair of wings upright and another pair, more prone, that formed a garment made of feathers.

In the midst of these beings presented another sight—one that made poor Ezekiel pale as he gazed—something like burning coals of fire that called up the image of torches, darting back and forth among the living beings. The living beings ran to and fro like bolts of lightning. More remarkable, four living beings of another sort were nearby. They were out of reach for any description, but Ezekiel called them whirling wheels. Their appearance was like sparkling beryl, and it was as if one wheel was within the other, their rims lofty and awesome, full of eyes round about. Among all the things that flew, these wheels flew remarkably above the earth in a strange flight, moving not like birds that go round in flight, in a circle for their turn. No, these wheels could relentlessly turn and stop and break off fast in any course that they might be after. And they turned in this way because the spirits of the living beings were within the wheels.

Above the living beings there was something of an expanse like the gleam of crystal and something of a throne like lapis lazuli in appearance. There was a figure on the throne, the figure of a man. Ezekiel saw Him, delicate and dreadful, and could not look away. From the figure's loins upward, a substance and a fire was all around, and from His loins downward, something of a fire. Waves of radiance were all around Him, like the appearance of the rainbow on a rainy day; such was the appearance of the likeness of the glory of the Lord. And when Ezekiel's flesh had had enough of the sight, he fell before his God.

God spoke to Ezekiel there and commissioned him to tell His people of their sin and their redemption. Then the Spirit lifted Ezekiel up, and as he was lifted into the air, he heard a great rumbling, the sound of the living beings transporting the throne, saying as they flew, "Blessed be the glory of the Lord."

Ezekiel obeyed, and soon afterward he spoke to the people of the covenant, saying to them, "God says that when you were born, your navel cord was not cut. By some action of your own, you are still connected to your origin, for your father was an Amorite and your mother a Hittite. Nor were you washed with water after you were born, nor rubbed with salt, nor even wrapped in clothes as one clothes a newborn in her first wrap. Rather you were in some remissive effort thrown out into the field and treated like an abortion; you were abhorred on the day you were born. But I passed by you in the field and saw you squirming in your blood. I said to you while you were still in your blood, 'Live!' I then made you abundant and remarkable among the peoples of the earth, and in all respects I cared for you as you grew into a nation. When you became tall and reached the age for fine ornaments, your breasts were formed and your hair had grown. And when you were at the time of love, I spread My skirt over you and covered your nakedness, for you were naked and knew it not.

"I was as a mother to you and a father, even while you thought it not worthwhile to consider Me. I had made a covenant with you, so I bathed you with water and attended you. I anointed you with oil. I had not meant for you to be so proud when I, in my enthrallment, had wrapped you with fine linen and covered you with silk, when I adorned you with My ornaments and bracelets, a necklace and a ring, and even a crown for your delighted head. You were exceedingly beautiful, and you knew in yourself your given royalty. I made you what you longed to be, yet you had something hidden there when you related your beauty to yourself.

"I soon found you no longer at My side, as your face had turned toward your idols. And while you beforehand trusted in Me, you now promoted the worship of another. You had walked dreamlike, as if in your own delightful vision, for such was the new manner of your heart—and also your eyes, which had drawn eagerly toward those lusty Egyptians. I saw your fancy gait before the men of Assyria, when they pranced before you on their horses. You played harlotry with them and craved them when you should have been for your Husband.

"You made out even worse than a common harlot, because her gratification is for money, which she feels more than her feeling for men. But you did not even demand any money from the men. Instead, you had an awkward way of paying the men for your indulgence. Now let Me tell you the story of two women, two sisters, Oholah and Oholibah. The first represents Samaria and the second, Jerusalem. Oholah was also Mine, but she had left her loveliness along the banks of Assyria. While she was scattered there, she saw all the choice men of Assyria and saw in them reward when she lusted after them. When they poured themselves upon her, she quickly became as something dreary. Her nakedness was uncovered, and they slew her with the sword. Her soul was cleaved, and her name became a byword in the streets.

"When her sister Oholibah saw this, she thought she would do even worse. She was indifferent to the trouble of her sister. In her prowess, she saw and lured the Assyrians, saw them robust and strapping, desirable young men. Then I saw she was like her sister and of the same face in shame. Yet she didn't stop; she remembered how these foreign men were girded with their belts and their flowing turbans on their heads, upright like officers in splendor.

"Therefore, I'll treat you as one whom no nobleman would take. You'll be presumed upon by rogues and worthless men to whom I'll give you over. You've long since gone from Me; go now to your lovers. Let's see if they, once fair, will treat you fairly. You aren't as silver; rather you're the fateful dross of silver. Therefore, you're like waste that men carelessly throw aside.

"Meanwhile, it's not like your apparent priests and prophets mourn for you. Instead, they've laid their hands quite well on you and shrewdly violated you for their own sakes. Your leaders advance on you religiously and, in seeming generosity of deed, take from you your treasure. They deserve the name of predator, which in all its ways is after you, to devour you as prey. And your prophets, who sit outside My presence, lie round about and wait with calculated intent, as wolves.

"Nevertheless, I won't leave you in your proper regrets, but I'll relax My wrath and make with you a new covenant. You'll no longer be in your abhorred and dislocated state when I'll finally be able to stand you and forgive you for all that you have done."

Later the Lord spoke to Ezekiel, saying, "See, I look on My Israel as a widower, because I'm in the attitude of a husband.

Son of man, see, your wife is going to die; I'll take her away, the desire of your heart. I've found occasion to use her death as a sign. Therefore, you must make up what is wanting in this sign by imitating how Israel will grieve—in a harsh mood. When your wife is gone, you'll neither mourn nor weep with fitting bereavement; you'll instead contend against the movement of your tears when they would come out from your grief. You'll move your pain inward, groaning there in silence."

In the morning, Ezekiel's wife died, and when the people saw Ezekiel grieving mute for the loss of his wife, they asked him why he carried his mood into such silence. Was this the effort of a sign?

Ezekiel said to them, "The Lord has made me into a guide, and my behavior into a sign, because the delight of your hearts will be taken from you, your sons, and your daughters by the sword. In that time, you'll grieve as I'm grieving. Your pangs will be in silence, and you'll rot away in your iniquities, and you'll groan in quiet to each other."

The Lord said to them, "I know you think this is unfair, but keep in mind during this woeful time that I have no delight in the death of the wicked. But in the space of time, I'll be like a shepherd, resolved to seek out his sheep among the scattered. I'll bring them out, all fresh, as one might pluck a flower from a thistle bush. I'll have in My hour much mercy, and grace will find you when I bind up all the broken and give strength to the sick. I have ready a new covenant of peace, a saving one, and a choice Shepherd who will feed the sheep—one like David."

Chapter 18

——— ⸱✳⸱ ———

It followed that Nebuchadnezzar, king of Babylon, besieged Jerusalem and took it. To raise the height of his kingdom, he asked for a few choice men of Israel to be introduced into the confines of his noblemen. Therefore, many exclusive youth were brought in, those without defect, who not only were good-looking but had some possession of intelligence in branches of wisdom and science, those who could be potentially charged to serve the standard of the king's court.

Among the sons of Judah were Daniel, Hananiah, Mishael, and Azariah, and these were brought up consequently for three years before the king. By the imprint of devotion or some other good within, Daniel and his friends were inspired to abstain from the easy lasciviousness that their promotion offered. The friends made up their minds not to eat of the king's choice food, in that they wished to be clean and for their God indeed. The commander of the officials who had charge over these adept men, was approving toward their behavior, yet he feared that without the choice food, their faces would show the withering fatigues of a constrained fast. Daniel and his friends adjured the favor of the commander to see with a sort of test whether their faces would confess conspicuously their lesser diet made of water and vegetables. The commander agreed, and for ten days they were tested to see.

After ten days, Daniel and his three friends looked healthier compared to their meat-eating cohorts, those who yielded themselves to the wine and meat. When the commander saw that Daniel and the three were brighter in their face, and healthier, he allowed them to keep their apparently abject diet.

As for these four youths, God gave them a bloom of knowledge in literature and in all branches of wisdom, and to Daniel He gave a broad scope of mind that could even interpret visions and dreams.

It happened in the second year of the reign of Nebuchadnezzar that the king had a dream. The dream protruded much, so that the king tossed about in his bed with indisposition. When he woke, the dream troubled him, and he could not make himself sure of it. He called his wise men to his feet—the magicians, the conjurers, the sorcerers, and the Chaldeans—that they might give light to it.

Nebuchadnezzar decided, by way of some species of distrust, to hide the dream from them. Instead, he said they ought to take their apparent skill and magic and tell him the dream and what it meant. In joint rank, the wise men said they were unable to see so far, that the king should rather bring the dream out into the open, and then they should know from where it came and make meaning from its figures. But the king was furious with them and threatened to strike them with death, saying, "You don't know the dream, and you have no clever answer. Therefore you are delaying for time, because you've surely set your minds together, and your whispering lips, to make up something when I tell you the dream."

Therefore the king was very upset and ordered all the wise men, the magicians, the sorcerers, and the Chaldeans to be killed. News of the disturbance reached Daniel, who, from a motive of survival and faith or confidence in God, asked the king for time that he might find an answer for the king. Daniel was then in his room and was in a deep mood to have the dream revealed to him by God. That night, a vision shone into Daniel's sleep and showed him what the king had dreamed. Daniel praised God and was hastily brought before Nebuchadnezzar. The king accepted Daniel before him and asked petulantly, because he was still in an awful humor, "Can you give me the dream and its answer?"

"I can," answered Daniel, "because there's a God in heaven who knows all things, and no thought too deep is concealed from Him. You saw, as you were looking out at night, something of a great and burly statue, and it had a great growth, and because of its splendor you could not help but heed to it in sight. With this augment the statue stood: its head in the splendor of fine gold, its breast and arms covered as in the smoothness of silver, its thighs and belly of bronze, its legs in shafts of iron, and its feet a mixture, here and there, of iron and of clay. And when you looked, oh king, toward the mountainside, toward the ground behind, a stone was cut out of it, which came rolling down and struck the figure of the statue and by crushing force reduced the statue to mere chaff. And whatever survived as chaff, the wind picked up and took it to a dust. Thereupon the stone grew large and heaved up into enormous size and entered its proportion into the entire earth.

"You, oh king, are the head of gold, so high that gold pervades your state, because the God of heaven has given you such a glory, such a strength, that wherever you may gaze over the lives of peoples and beasts, you gaze as one who rules exceedingly. Something with less glory follows your reign, a second kingdom that is silver, and after that another, even less than you, yet great, not bleak, in the manner of the bronze. After the bronze another kingdom will rule and look out over all the earth, one composed of iron, inasmuch as iron imitates a crushing strength. Last follow the feet and toes, which impressed you with its mixture, some of clay and some of iron. The peoples of the feet correspond thus in mixture, mixing not their seeds with one another."

History lights up the metaphor and can interpret silver as the kingdom of the Medes and Persians, bronze as the fair life of the Greeks, when they in their time thrived, and iron as the severity of the Roman Empire. What remained of the Roman Empire, when it could not rely on the legs for cohesive strength, resulted in a splattering of dominions and unaccustomed clay. As for the overcoming stone, Daniel hinted at an entirely new kingdom, set up by God and, therefore, mystic, triumphant, and eternal.

Now when king Nebuchadnezzar heard the dream and its interpretation, he was amazed, and being unable to defend his pride or anger, he fell down before Daniel and praised Daniel's God.

Time went on, and it must have pleased Nebuchadnezzar to know that he was considered a "golden" roof over all of man, and his pride could not shut the picture out. Therefore he set his sights on public adulation by building a golden statue of himself and forcing the exultation of the populace. A decree was made that, whenever the musicians made music at the statue, all the people should in the name of it fall down and accept the gloating figure as something of a god. The pernicious effect of this awful worship betrayed the religious Jews, specifically Daniel's three friends, who had airily refused to trust the golden stone.

A few opportunistic Chaldeans, who hated the Jews, went before the king. "Had you not, oh king, compelled all people to obey in steady salutation the golden form of you? But now there are these three—Shadrach, Meshach, and Abed-nego—who thought differently of your rule, because they have surely set their minds on another trust and shape: their own god."

To the king, this was a slight, and he was very angry. He called forward the three and implied to them severity if they refused to bow to the statue, by the threat of an awesome fire.

It is supposed that a furnace was kept by the king, wherein whole persons could be thrown—something needful to keep things pliant, the actuating force of law. The fiery furnace was not ominous enough for the steadfast three men, and they replied to the indignant king that they must disdain the golden figure with their lives. There was then much kindling within the king, and also in the furnace, because the king commanded for the flame to be lit seven times more than its usual blazing heat. The three young men were thrown inside. However they were tossed, the guards who did the throwing died; such was the power of the fire.

The king attended the intended burning of the men, but his feeling of justice and vindication changed suddenly while he watched the scene. He asked around, saying, "Weren't three men meant for the sacrifice? How come I see *four*—and the fourth one is flaming like a son of God?"

The marvelous sight made the bewildered king run in haste near to the entrance of the furnace, and he called out, "Shadrach, Meshach, and Abed-nego, servants of the Most High God, come out!"

Many of the officials gathered around to see the three unharmed. In a pitched voice, the astounded Nebuchadnezzar declared on the spot that this God should be of concern and that whoever might by doubt this God demean should be with sharp things cut into pieces.

Time has weeds that do the flowers in, and the king in time forgot about his decree and his astonishment, and he presumed to hold out in pride. It happened awhile later, when he was having himself preferable and aloof and at great ease, that another dream intruded into his mind. This dream was of a great tree that surpassed all others, for its towering size and its branches spread out over all the earth, and from its shade it looked down on the prosperity of its abundance. In the dream, also, some bright lord appeared, an angelic watcher descending down from heaven, shouting loud into the air, saying, "Cut down the tree and its fellow branches, but waste not the stump; for thereon will be a band of iron and bronze placed, and when the new grass of the field appears, let the stump feed on the grass as a mindless beast might feed and strive and be drenched in the open fields. This is a command of the holy one in order that the living might know that the Most High is ruler over all of mankind and bestows rule unto whomsoever He wishes."

Therefore, it was again occasion for the king to lean on the advice of the magicians, but none of them knew what to say of the dream or its interpretation. Then came Daniel before the king. Daniel had something of a reservation when he answered the king, knowing that the king would not be better off.

"The surpassing tree is you, oh king," said Daniel, "you who rule in this assuming figure. There has been a demand for your repentance, inasmuch as you will be like the trunk, cut off from your lofty state, and you'll be for seven years in a hard state, being made soft and lowly as a beast. The hint is in the grass, because something will clasp your very mind, and you shall lose all expectation and all sense, and senseless roam from field to field. Therefore, oh king, perhaps you might extend your prosperity. Make quickly a new life, live around repentance, and live toward the poor."

Now it came to pass twelve months later, when the king was in a comfortable mood on his patio, overlooking all his splendor, that his pernicious pride crept in, which produced his fall. No sooner had he turned his eyes toward his dilated state, when a voice sounded from heaven, saying, "King Nebuchadnezzar, sovereignty has been removed from you!"

By this word he was immediately spoiled, and he was driven out like a beast, banished for his madness away from mankind. He did not know that he was eating grass, thinking it not mad; nor was he troubled by his likeness or the growing of his hair, when it was at last thick and woven like the feathers of a bird, or his nails that became set like the claws of a bird. For seven years he lived in the likeness of an animal. Then he somehow turned his eyes toward heaven and saw his own depressed life and saw something of the height of God. Thereupon his reason returned, and he gave recognition and honor to the Most High God. With this epiphany, the errant king strode back into the city, where some of his officials took him and restored him back to his kingly consecration. In time he died, and at length his son took his place.

King Belshazzar, the son and heir of the seat, afforded himself much luxury. He acquired in the moment of a great feast the terrible idea of drinking wine from the gold vessels of the temple of Jerusalem. These dedicated vessels had been taken from their shrine in the time of Nebuchadnezzar. Belshazzar had the mind to make frivolity with his wine and the vessels, and he poured wine for his officials and his concubines. With delight he was musing in this way, and sipping and praising the gods of gold and silver. Suddenly a dreadful hand appeared out of thin air, writing on the wall, all by itself, the words: MENE, MENE, TEKEL, UPHARSIN.

The king saw the apparition with a whimpering gaze and could not explain it in any way. As for the strength of his body, it did not help, and his hips and knees sank away, and his face felt how a pale face might feel. At once there was consternation, because his nobles and his concubines saw the hand as well and were perplexed and in a lame pause.

Many a diviner was rushed in to give an answer to this aspect, but they could do nothing. When the queen heard of the commotion, she entered in, saying to King Belshazzar, "Oh king, live forever. There is a man who has the spirits of the holy gods, who fares well with secrets. Your father, even king Nebuchadnezzar, had appointed him chief of the magicians, because there was an extraordinary spirit within him."

The composed interposition of the queen settled things down, and Daniel was brought in before king Belshazzar. Reverence or fear of the king might have induced a polite interpretation of the ghostly writing, but Daniel said outright to the king, "It says this: Your kingdom has been numbered, and you've been weighed and found wanting. Your kingdom is divided and given over to the Medes and Persians."

That night the king had his last night's sleep, because he was assassinated in the dark, and Darius the Mede received the kingdom in his place.

Darius had in the course of his reign felt it wise to appoint a hundred and twenty satraps over the kingdom, and over them three higher, commissioners, of whom Daniel was one. Now evil lies not still in man and cannot for long lie low within the hollows of the heart; sooner or later it seeks to blow out its dark air in spouts that opportunity affords. Darius had meant to promote Daniel over all the rest because he had an extraordinary spirit in him, but when the satraps and the other commissioners took note of the promotion, they were distraught with jealousy. They peered about for a fault in Daniel's state and work but could not find enough to close their trap around. "We can't put our hands on him through fault, because he doesn't do much trouble. Perhaps we can trick him through his god, and subject him in that way."

In seeming tepidness, they proposed a law that had—they told the naive Darius—no other cause than for the honor of the king, that for thirty days no prayers should otherwise be raised except to the king himself. Darius sealed the law, being unaware that the apparent complimentary fragment of law was meant for conspiracy. Then these men watched and waited to seize good Daniel in his private deed. Daniel's devotion promised more to him than the risk of disobedience to a perverse decree, and when Daniel maintained his faithful pattern to pray to God, the satraps had the bad grin of triumph in their teeth. They waited for an opportune time outside Daniel's door, pulsing for their eager sakes, and then as might the figure of a thief at night through a window creep, they stole right in and caught him on his knees.

The effect of their catch made them walk stuffed-up to the king, saying, "Did you not say that the people could pray to no one else? See, this Daniel was holy for another one; therefore you must consider him in light of the ways of the Medes and Persians and make no excuse when you throw him into the lion's den."

The distraught Darius accepted the condemnation on the grounds of his decree, yet privately he sought to search through the laws that he might touch on an escape. Darius groped around all night in this way and was frustrated that, when all things were under him, he was under himself. The satraps had their revelry when Daniel was no longer part of their share, because he was for food thrown to the lions.

King Darius was no able sleeper that night, and in the morning he was conscious still of Daniel. Early the next morning at dawn, he went to the den of lions and cried out, "Daniel, has the god whom you serve saved you from your death?"

Then he heard Daniel's voice calling back behind the stone—because the den was sealed deliberately tight—saying, "Oh king, my God sent His angel last night to my aid, which has shut the lions' mouths. This because my God has acknowledged my innocence. I've not done any crime."

The excited king Darius found his voice in spite of his surprise and was then shouting as a man in haste, ordering that Daniel be brought out at once. The king, as if vindicated, ordered the satraps to be themselves thrown likewise into the den. When they were thrown, the hungry lions took them even while they were in the air.

Daniel was consequently much regarded and was safe and successful in the circle of King Darius and also during the time of King Cyrus, the Persian.

One day as Daniel was on his bed awake, something lit inside his head, and a sudden vision and insight bloomed, wherein there were the comings and goings of kingdoms and of kings—man and time being yet in their incipient buds, because it was an end-time sight of humanity. Daniel saw a dark hour of a dark king who thought it not audacity to speak bravely against God. Daniel saw thrones being set up, and the Ancient of Days on His. The glorious sight of the Most High prevailed upon Daniel as he looked into the vision, seeing God's vesture in the brightness of white snow and His hair as white as perfect wool. His throne was full of flames, all ablaze. As for this throne, it had a fire turning, a river—not of water but of blaze—surging and pouring out from the throne. The majesty of the scene included thousands and thousands who gave themselves to Him and myriads upon myriads who stood before the glory of the throne. These holy ones had held their songs and bows, and did thereby no wrong, because this summoning of the hosts was for the reason of a judgment, and it had the silence of a court.

The court sat and books were opened. A review was done of a future day and of an abominable king and his awful ambition to search out for boastful blasphemies against the Most High. In the vision, Daniel saw the outcome: this king—or beast, as he was figured in—was slain and his body destroyed and his soul given to a burning fire.

Daniel kept looking through the gleam of the night vision and the opened books and saw the clouds of heaven, which were myriads upon myriads of holy ones. There was One coming through and with the holy throng, one like the Son of Man. This particular Man came up to the Ancient of Days and was presented before Him and made distinct. An effusion of favor radiated the air, and this Son of Man was esteemed and granted kingdoms and glory, and He was given the delight and privilege of everlasting dominion.

Daniel saw all these but was confused and unable to sensibly describe the picture of the coming events in simple terms. Therefore, while still in the vision, he approached one of the holy ones who was standing around in order that he might come to some conclusion about the progress of the figures. The holy one, an angel, explained for Daniel's sake that the abominable king, exceedingly dreadful, like a beast with teeth of iron and claws of bronze, would face the saints of God, devouring and overcoming them until the Ancient of Days stepped in as the agent of their hope. At that time, the saints of the Highest One would take possession of the kingdom.

In the third year of the reign of Belshazzar (before he was slain), Daniel was for the sake of another vision transported to Susa, to the canal of Ulai. As Daniel was looking out on the water, he saw a ram. This ram had two horns and was boldly standing in front of the canal. The ram had the felicity of strength and was butting westward, northward, and southward, and no other beast could take the ram on for its range, nor oppose it for its strength. From the west, a shaggy male goat appeared for doom. The goat had a single strength, a single horn between its eyes. The goat's wrath surpassed its fear, and it came up, moving fast—so fast that its hooves were set in air within its gallop, touching not the earth for the fury of its storm. Out and gone the old ram was, because the goat hit it on the side, and the wild ram's horns were off; indeed the horns and ram were by the goat entirely disposed.

No sooner was the goat in victory when it magnified itself remarkably and revered itself without censure. The duration of its gloating state contracted, because the conspicuous horn was broken off somehow. Nonetheless, out of the left-over trunk of the horn grew out four little horns, and from one of the four, another baby horn began to peak. This little horn made for a marvelous perspective to the seeing eye: it grew exceedingly large toward the south and east and toward the Beautiful Land. It preferred also, in some sort of pride and wicked strength, to grow up to the hosts of heaven, causing some of the angelic stars to fall down to the earth, where it trampled them down. Within the glow of Daniel's vision, a holy one appeared, an angel in the form of a man; and another holy one was across, calling out to this one, saying, "Gabriel, give this man the understanding of the vision."

Gabriel came up close, and Daniel would rather have been alone because he could no longer hold his fear, and he fell, frightened, on his face. With a hospitable hand, the great angel touched Daniel's soul, helping him against the last struggles of his human force, and made him stand upright.

"The ram," Gabriel said, "with the two horns, are the kings of Media and Persia, and the shaggy goat that mustered so successfully is the kingdom of Greece, and its large, single horn is its king. This king will remain for a short time and will leave behind only an incohesive glory—the growing of four lesser kingdoms from its base. In the last days of these tempered kingdoms, when they're all weak, another branch will grow—the little baby horn, growing tumultuously with horrid limbs, even as a stretching tree lifts itself indifferent to the plantings on its sides. The king of this careless kingdom will hide his skill and scheme, and the nearby kingdoms won't see his insolence because of the skill of his intrigue. He'll come not as an interceding lord, nor as a green bower for a shade; he's no understanding father nor a kind mother. He saw this all as faults and intrusions for his plan to prey on the entire world. Within his rakish heart sits a corresponding evil spirit, a frog that causes him to swell and even to oppose the Prince of princes. To that achievement, he won't have strength enough to succeed, and God will see him broken, breaking him without the use of human help."

Chapter 19

— ❧✖❧ —

Meanwhile God kept prophesying of future events through the prophets. He spoke through the prophet Joel, trying to get the people's attention and heart. At the time of Joel, the Israelites had run to their own corners and had contracted to the recesses of their little residues because they had, through the years, loosened themselves from the covenant they had made with God. They saw God's litanies in the light or treatment of indifferent philosophy or distant history—and therefore as not real. They perversely preferred to kiss the forehead of an idol at the shrines of wood and stone.

Whatever counsel they got for their sakes from the lifeless deities, they could not watch out for the wrath of the law, and God reminded them of this tiding, how it was blowing against their state, saying, "A consuming intruder has gathered and is coming to your end to finish you off entirely in your last and dismal hours. Though it be enough for the gnawing locusts to take your greens, the swarming locusts will move in hungering behind them; and what the swarming locusts leave behind, the creeping locusts will eat up next. And if there be any left of the bitter feast, the stripping locusts will know how to finish it all off. Still, there will be a particular day, a day of darkness and gloom, of clouds and thick darkness, a particular day I wish to awake you to by My angel's trumpet, to shake you from your drunken way.

Afterward, I'll have pity on you all. I'm going to satisfy you in an abundant way; and after this it will come about that I'll pour out My Spirit on all mankind. It will therefore also be an amazing day, the great day of the Lord, because in that day there will be enough sweet wine to suit the mountains, even to the point of overflow, when the mountains drip with sweet wine; nor will the hills pass on the indulgence of abundance, because even they will flow like no day before with streams of milk."

As for Israel, God's admonitions and promises fell short of the immediate hope of the people, and they, for their evil, hoped preferably in the old fires of their wickedness—the passionate days of lasciviousness and cruelty and idols.

God went on through the prophet Amos, saying to His people, "Will you continue in these tired idols? If only you would wake up! But you're walking around as in the madness of a sleepwalker. Therefore you insensibly oppress the poor and do much other wickedness, calling forth to your husbands, saying to them, 'Remember to bring us wine. Let's have a rowdy time tonight!' It's amazing to Me that even when you were confounded by My plagues, by which you have been blasted, you still walk so confidently in your uncertain state. By the same means, I've done many things to you, imputing to you your sins in order to satiate the demands of the Law—except that I had hoped you might return to Me. Yet your were pert to Me in your response. You have faked turning to Me, as though you were trying Me with a trick. Don't you know that I'm after you for your heart and not for your disaster? You are to Me, in a way, like the sadness of Sodom. When the brimstone comes, I have to pull you out ahead, pull you like a firebrand from the burning heap. If I had not this heart in Me, My heart of love, I would've mastered you a long time ago and consumed you for your sins.

"I see there are a few of you who muster up a strange strength, and in your uncertain minds you try to please Me with your boring and laborious work. You give Me strange service with your assemblies when you give Me burned offering and grain offerings and fattened offerings for peace. When you sing songs to Me or make music to Me with your instruments, I should rather wish you to stop, because your labor turns it into unbearable noise. Indeed, it's not yet time for Me to give My grace, so therefore there are now left only curses for your cries. Really, when you bring to Me your rituals and try to conjure Me to your guilty side, do you think these can truly emulate My loving heart? You're impaired by your unfamiliarity of Me, and you wish to augment your ignorance with works, even knowing that I'm not after the pattern of the imperfect and that imperfect works can't be considered for the standard of perfection. So off with you and your backbreaking deeds; you can't conquer My heart with your hand nor negate My holiness with the vigor of your tries. Nonetheless, don't lose hope. There's a better thing coming, because there will be a day when I will, by My own strength and with joy, rebuild the tent of David, rebuild it as in times past, and what now appears as waste will be instead an acceptable overflow."

Now the Lord took the prophet Jonah and said to him, "Go say something decisive against the city of Nineveh, because their fierce wickedness has come up before Me."

Jonah would not hear the command, and for the heaviness of it sought out a release therefrom. Jonah thought the gust of a sea wind might be faster than the gaze of God and the reach of guilt, and he fled, paying the fare for a ship bound for Tarshish.

Peace could not be had by this attempted distance or speed, and God was concerned for the lives of the people in Nineveh. So God sent an overlooking wind that hung, brooding over the tossing of the little ship. The sailors and the men worked as a wild crowd to compose the ship, throwing about the cargo so that the ship might by their attempts stay straight. But conscience or superstition told them of a possible instrument of their impending loss: that one of those aboard was the cause of their fate. Therefore they consulted the credulous wisdom of a lot, casting it among themselves, and it fell on Jonah. Each man had meantime prayed to his god, but to no avail, and when by reason of the lot they blamed their struggles on Jonah, they asked him who he was and how come a fury was sent against the ship.

"I'm a Hebrew, and my God is the God of heaven, the one who made the sea and land, and I'm fleeing from Him."

When they heard this, they more confidently blamed the intent of the storm on Jonah, and they were very much terrified. The force of their concern stirred the placid Jonah to the obvious solution, and he said to the sailors, "Take me up and throw me overboard, that my God may no longer have you in His sight."

The men were reluctant and tried to drive on with their weary oars. The cause of the storm was not abated, and at length the men took the silent Jonah and flung him to the waves. They were greatly astonished afterward, because the storm sank softly into the waves, and the waves left off leaping from their hollows. As for Jonah, he was pulled down by sea, vanquished underneath, sinking to the misery of the bottom of the water. The billows and the waves and even the weeds wrapped around poor Jonah. His reluctance or distance to God remained, in spite of his watery state, and he would have drowned in silence and without dispute. Yet the Lord sent a great fish that swallowed him alive. Inside the fish, Jonah overcame his stubbornness or self-pity and finally prayed. The Lord answered and spoke to the fish, and after three days it vomited Jonah out on dry land. All this shaking about made Jonah insensibly assiduous to the obedience of the word of God, and he went walking through the city of Nineveh, crying out, "In forty days it will be over for this city!"

The king of Nineveh learned of the coming doom and was no longer in his pastime but tried to avert the hand of God. He declared for his people a great fast, that they should put their meanness behind them, clothe themselves in sackcloth, and not eat or drink—that they might by chance presume on the mercy of this God. Even their cattle were regarded in the way of the fast and were covered with sackcloth and given nothing to eat. The quivering animals knew not what to make of the peculiar fast, and the people knew not whether their toilsome effort might work for sorrow or for joy. God saw that the people placed enough efforts on their regrets, and a vestige of grace could overrule the demands of perfection. He relented and spared the city.

Jonah was now left without a consequence, and he was moaning much in spite, saying to God, "See now why I fled from you, because I knew You are gracious and merciful, slow to anger, abundant in love and kindness. You never wish to do harm; therefore I knew all this when I ran from you. There was no point for me to even walk around and work these people up. Now what will they think of me? I should rather just be dead!"

So Jonah crossed over to the east side of the city, sat down, and ruminated miserably in the heat of the sun. God was aware of the heat and of Jonah's misery, and He grew a plant to the side of Jonah that could provide shade for Jonah's head. The miraculous growth soothed Jonah, and he was very happy about the plant. The next day, Jonah sat up, perplexed, because God had sent a worm to eat the plant, to dwindle it to its stem. And Jonah said again, "It is better for me to be dead."

"Is it right for you to be angry over the loss of the plant?" God asked him.

"Yes, it is," said Jonah, sulking.

God answered sympathetically, "You are right to consider the plant and your well-being, but shouldn't I have an interest in one hundred and twenty thousand people of the city and many animals?"

Chapter 20

— ❧ ✖ ❧ —

Meanwhile, God continued to have a difficult time esteeming His people dear, not for His heart but for His holiness; therefore, He was eager to set up His marvelous redemptive plan for mankind, formed even before the foundation of the world. It was no paltry thing for Him to use the words of prophets in declaring His bold interests. He needed their words, as it were, for creating again, even in His rest. His motive was to create again by words, words made up by men, because He was bound by His own words when He gave mankind the earth, that they should have authority thereover, inasmuch as they had full dominion of it. If anything new would enter earth, it had to come by men. For four thousand years, God patiently collected certain words of man, that He might even by their faith and words create again—not something from the seeds of things that by innate law spawn what exists, but something new by a new means, not after the fallen vigor of fallen things. No, it must be a new Seed that had survived the mortal curse because it was distinguished in Itself, being eternal and outside of the confounded state of natural man. The promise therefore was of a new species of man that would appear by means of a body of a man.

God then keenly used more prophets to speak forth into being His new Man. No single prophet could stand well within the awful gap, and each prophet was not full enough, even when he or she groped about and groaned with pieces of prophetic sights.

The method needed the perfect compilation of a strenuous effort of faith and words. It took four thousand years for the prattle of the wicked to be restrained and to be outdone by the faith and words of the prophets.

The prophet Micah added his auxiliary words and faith, and he declared in public the place—Bethlehem, and the tribe of Judah—out of which would come the manifestation of the One, the Ruler whose comings and goings were even told of old and from the everlasting. Micah told of Israel who was in labor, ready to give birth to a manifestation.

By the prophet Habakkuk came words that were a prologue or a pattern of the future way, a vision for a destined time of something marvelous and almost strange—that the just would live by faith. Therein too lay hope in the attitude of strength, because God would make the people's feet like the feet of a deer that could skip on high hills.

And by Haggai, God spoke of something to be glad of: that there would come far more of a glory than what was, that the glory of the new house would be greater than the glory of the old house.

By Zechariah, He said how fair He was toward the daughter of Zion, that He would be drawing in a single day nations to her midst, for He would live in her. Now the Lord showed Zechariah something of the future and something marvelous. Through Zechariah's vision, God showed Zechariah a high priest called *Jesus*—translated "Joshua" in the Hebrew tongue—standing tall within the scene. Zechariah saw Jesus clothed in soiled rags. Now there was something awful to the sight, because on Jesus' right hand, Satan stood preferred, accusing Him on account of the rags that represented the sin of mankind. And Satan stood there opposing Him.

The Lord said to Satan, "The Lord rebuke you, Satan! This brand has been plucked from the fire."

In the vision, the repose of Jesus changed, because God viewed Jesus' burden as a great accomplishment through a perilous crossing, and as having accomplished perfection, and God commanded the angels, "Take away the filthy dress. See, I've taken away iniquity from Him. Clothe Him with clean clothes, and give Him a crown of silver and gold, that those who love Him can see His glory. In the success of perfection, He will sit and rule upon His throne, and peace will be between Me and Him. Be glad, daughter of Zion, because your King has come down diminished, riding on a donkey, lowly, on a colt. He'll come in this way to His children, and He brings with Him salvation. And when I have accomplished My means, I'll pour out My Spirit of grace, and they'll look upon Me whom they have pierced for blood. Awake, O sword; this is not a dream. Awake against My Shepherd, against My Friend, and have your splendid strike. 'Look, He is coming,' says the Lord of hosts, 'and I'll send My messenger ahead of Him when He arrives on earth.'"

It happened in the days of the Roman empire, in the days of Herod, that a certain man—a priest named Zacharias, a righteous man—was burning incense in the temple of the Lord. He had no children, and his wife, Elizabeth, was old. Zacharias was suddenly frightened because there at the altar's side appeared an angel. The angel said to him, "Don't be afraid, because your wife's barrenness is not for nothing now. See, she'll bear a son and you'll name him John. The Lord will be his object, and he'll go about for Him, making the people prepared, making a way for His coming."

Neither the angel's prophetic claim nor Zacharias' good heart were sufficient teachers of faith, and Zacharias replied to the angel, "But how can this be?"

It seemed Zacharias' unbelief deserved the impatience of the angel, who declared, "I am Gabriel who stands in the presence of God, and what I said will nonetheless come true; but as for you, you will be mute. Only when the child comes forth will you have had enough of silence."

About six months later, Gabriel went to Nazareth, a city of Galilee, to a virgin called Mary, who was betrothed to Joseph. Now Joseph had passed from the loins of Abraham. Fourteen generations prevailed between Abraham and David, and fourteen more from David to Joseph and his son, the Christ. Coming in Mary's room, Gabriel said, "Greetings, favored one! The Lord is with you, and look! You'll conceive in your womb and bear a son, and you'll name Him Jesus. It's finally He, the Son of the Most High!"

Mary did not get lost in the dazzling scene, nor in humbleness did she deem herself unworthy. She only asked the angel how it could be, for she was not yet with a man.

Gabriel answered her, "The Holy Spirit will overshadow you and will release at once all the words of the prophets throughout the ages. Therefore the One who is coming forth will be the very Son of God."

Some time afterward Mary decided to go see her relative Elizabeth. The baby within Elizabeth needed nothing else and leapt when Mary entered and gave her greeting. At that moment, John, being still in Elizabeth's womb, was filled with the Holy Spirit. In due season, Elizabeth gave birth to the baby boy. The birth was surrounded by the suspense and curiosity of the people close by, because they disturbed the parents for the child's name, that it should be after his father, a custom of the time.

Elizabeth answered, "No, he shall be John."

The unrelenting people made signs to Zacharias, as he was still mute, asking him whether he had no ambition for the heritage of his name and that of his son. To this Zacharias answered by means of a writing tablet, "His name is John." And instantly Zacharias' voice was loosed, and he praised God, and the people marveled.

John grew and became strong in his spirit and spent his time where the winds were, in the desert and with God. It was also the time of Caesar Augustus, who was in search of his people to have them register by means of a census and a forced decree.

Joseph and Mary took care of the census by going to Bethlehem, because Joseph was of the house of David. There were many people bustling about, and few would hear the cry of the baby born. Mary could give the Child no more than a manger, because the inn was full, and the other people did not care.

Meanwhile, upon the faces of some shepherds in the field came the circumstance of fright, because, as they were huddling at night idly around their fires and their flocks, an angel came with all his glare, saying to the prostrate group, "I bring you good news, which is for all people, for today is born the Christ! This will be the sign: a baby in a manger."

The announcement caused heaven and thousands of angels, by the force of joy, to break forth into visible sight; and in that stunning moment, the shepherds saw the great hosts, the angels in their rapture. From their state came, composed, the declaring chorus of words, "Glory to God in the highest, and on earth peace between God and man, with whom He is pleased!"

After a needful time of fright and perusal, the shepherds said to each other, "Let's go see what this is all about."

Within the limits of distance and haste, they rushed toward Bethlehem and found the Child and were not modest in their acclamations, saying to all those around what was encouraged by the angel and the hosts.

After Jesus was born, Mary and Joseph followed the proper guidance of the law of Moses, to turn with their Child this way and that according to what the law had fixed. They did the best they could, making some time later a journey back to Jerusalem to present Jesus there before God, as it was written that every firstborn male that opened the womb should be consecrated to the Lord.

There was during this time a man who lived in Jerusalem who was called Simeon, in whose faith and fidelity God saw righteousness, and even recompense, because God promised him no slender hope, saying to him that he would not be too old to see the promised One. Coming in at that very time, Simeon saw the Child brought in by Joseph and Mary, and taking Him into his arms with awe, he said, "Now, Lord, You can take me up, for I've seen what you've made for our peace; I've seen Your salvation, a Child for our sake, a light of revelation to the Gentiles and the glory of Your people Israel."

The unready Mary and Joseph took it all in, being not sure yet what to make of their Messiah, only that they should keep it in their hearts. There was another who arrived at the consecration: Anna, a prophetess who was very old, yet who prayed day and night with her life apart. Coming in at that moment, she saw the Child and spoke of how He would live, how He would be for salvation.

Jesus grew in wisdom and grace. When He was twelve years old, He and His family went back to Jerusalem for the feast of Passover. After the days and conditions of the feast were over, the family and their caravan returned home, but the Boy Jesus asserted Himself there, lingering behind in Jerusalem, and His parents knew it not, supposing He had simply mingled in amongst the train of the caravan. After a day, His parents no longer understood His absence and tried to gather Him from their acquaintances. Their search was converted into anxiety, and they returned back to Jerusalem with distressed resolve, where they found Him three days later sitting in the temple. In this picture they saw Him listening to the teachers and asking them revolving questions. To the teachers indulgence and astonishment, He answered their knowledge remarkably well. His parents were amazed when they saw Him, saying to Him, "Son, why have You done this to us? We were very worried!"

He returned, "Why were you looking for Me? I must do what My Father wants."

But His parents were confounded and returned with Him to Nazareth, where He subjected Himself to them.

Chapter 21

—⊰ ✖ ⊱—

It was the fifteenth year of Tiberius Caesar, with Pontius Pilate the governor of Judea and Herod the tetrarch of Galilee. Looming also in this time were the dark shadows of two white-washed figures, Annas and Caiaphas, the notorious and fateful high priests of the Jews. None of these men could with their dark eyes see the Dawn. As for the Day, it did not arrive with thundering incident but rather through the gradation of a steady proclamation—this through the method of a desert prophet who started calling out as Isaiah had predicted, "A voice in the wilderness that prepares the way of the Lord, a path that is made straight. And if there will be hollow valley in His way, it shall be filled, or a mountain foot intrusive, it shall be made away; and for the crooked places, a repair, and the rough places, a plateau. Indeed, all mankind will see the salvation of God."

John, however peculiar he was, living in the desert on honey and locusts, approached from time to time from the desert and started a ritual of baptism. The Jews of the time participated in this repentance, passing humbly through the water in reverence to God, or perhaps in bemusement of John. John's reputation grew, and the people pondered whether he might be the promised Christ. This was not an unusual thought, given the Jewish culture of the time. The Jewish people and their teachers, in spite of their ignorance and the shortness of their capricious temper—for they had killed off most of their own prophets through the ages—were rightly aware of a promised savior. Therefore, it was no wonder when they caught sight of John, a man who displayed himself unfettered to the interest of his God and to peculiarity, that they leaned toward that curiosity of mind. John answered them that he was not the savior, but that he in fact was at the feet of the coming One, whose sandal strap he was not worthy to loose, and that this One coming would not in the same way use water to baptize but would baptize with the Spirit and with fire. This One would having a winnowing fan in His hand, and also zeal, to clean out the threshing floor for wheat that went to His barn and for chaff that went to a horrible flame.

One day as John was baptizing the crowds, he spotted Jesus walking on the riverbank. He exclaimed, "Behold the Lamb of God!"

Now Jesus had come to be baptized by John, but John said to Him, "It's best for You to baptize me, not the other way around."

Jesus answered, "Nonetheless, baptize Me for completion's sake."

From the water, Jesus rose up by the hand of John, and from above the Holy Spirit flew on Him in the manner of a bird when it alights, in the manner of a dove in its perching approach. A voice from the heavens called out at the same moment, saying, "You're My beloved Son in whom I'm well pleased!"

The crowd heard the voice, but in their confusion they invented it to be the muffled rumble of distant thunder.

Meanwhile, the terrible Satan had insensibly prowled around, because he had spent his days and all his strength on the lookout for the coming Seed. From his darkness, he was never quite sure which one through the ages would overthrow his reign, and in this way he had passed his days uncertain. When Satan heard reports that there was someone great around, he lingered near to scout Him out. No sooner had the great voice of God affirmed the Seed than Satan stirred himself with fright and hate to see how he might fool in any wicked way the promise made to Eve.

The Holy Spirit took Jesus immediately afterward to a wilderness, an arid place, for an awful match—the starting match for mankind's fate. One cannot reasonably describe the battle with soft, common senses but can only say that the Man had, as a man and not God, stood against the madness and temptations of the dark lord. He fasted for forty days and was for forty days thus tempted to weakness. The Christ stood as man would stand, in fallen flesh; yet He was distinct in this: His strength contained the lifted and untainted Spirit from above.

After forty days, Satan thought he should slay Him through His hunger, asking Him with words in shapes of doubt, "If you're the Son of God, command these stones into bread."

Jesus returned by saying, "Man doesn't live only by bread but by every word of God."

Then the Devil, more foul, more daring, took Jesus to something of a height within the spirit realm and showed Him the kingdoms of the world. Satan, being bold, proposed a trade, saying to Jesus, "All this authority was once delivered to me by Adam, even its glory; therefore I can fulfill your desire and give it to you. Only spend a moment in this trade on me: bow to me for the kingdom's sake, and it plainly will be yours."

Jesus answered, "Get behind Me, Satan, for it is written, you shall only worship the Lord your God."

Satan had not to his own hopes succeeded; therefore he took Jesus to Jerusalem and set Him on the pinnacle of the temple, saying, "If you're the Son of God, jump off here, because, see, it is written, 'He'll send His angels to keep you, to bear you up in their hands, to make sure you're not hurt from the fall.'"

Jesus answered, "You shall not tempt the Lord your God."

Many other temptations were tried by the Devil, but he could with none of them the Son of Man detain. Soon afterward, Jesus began to affect Himself with the people, teaching them in the synagogues. With a short word He announced Himself, taking the scroll of Isaiah, and read the stately passage, "The Spirit of the Lord is upon Me, because He has anointed Me to preach the good news to the poor, to heal the broken people, to proclaim freedom to those in bondage, sight to the blind, liberty for the oppressed, the acceptable year of the Lord."

"Today," Jesus concluded to them, "this word is fulfilled even in your hearing."

When He closed the book, He sat down, and everyone looked intently on Him. Now it was the custom in the synagogues to have an extra chair set out, placed under the expectation of the coming of the Messiah, He who would one day appear and take this reserved and empty seat. Through the years, the lonely chair had long been diverted to mere custom and had been reduced proportionally within the habitual mind to some far-off object. And when Jesus took the seat of the Messiah, the audience looked up at Him, wondering. In spite of this grand statement from Jesus, the people were not awakened to the times forecast by the prophets; they were only by the gentleness of His words enamored.

They said to each other, "Is He not Joseph's son?"

Jesus, meanwhile, understood that they were slow in rising from their sleep, thinking Him too familiar in their own eyes to be moved to the stature of the Messiah. Therefore He answered them, "Don't dismiss Me as a prophet too quickly, because I tell you that during the time of many widows, Elijah was sent to none of them except one; and in the time of Elisha, in the years of poverty and leprosy, he cleansed a single one."

This statement was apparently too forward for the crowd, and they capriciously rose up and took Him, without moderation and with a thrust to the brow of a nearby hill, that they might do away with Him. He was more boundless than they knew, and He walked away as if invisible from their midst.

Next He proceeded with ease to Capernaum and taught mostly what they could not comprehend, their fleshly minds kept their insights low. Nonetheless, the people of Capernaum were awed, as they saw Him teach with unusual authority. At some point in His teaching, the people suddenly gasped at Him—and at a man who had started foaming at the mouth, launching himself in wild animation, like a demon lashing out, for the man was possessed. With a seeming careless shout, the demon spewed to the Lord in great fear, "Leave us alone! What business do we have with You, Jesus of Nazareth? Have You come to destroy us? I know who You are—the Holy One of God!"

Jesus said, "Be quiet! Come out of the man!"

The demon tossed the man with several plunges down; it could not do much else against the power that forced it out.

When the sun was setting, late-born hope arose among the people, and they took their sick to Him. He laid His hands on all, and it hardly seemed unusual as they contentedly took their cures. And many demons fled, crying out, "You are the Son of God!"

One day He went out, presuming to repose in silence and in peace, but the tantalized crowd did not regard His quiet time and sought Him out to be with Him. He was not dependent on the people's aim, because they sought to keep Him with pleas and adulation. Instead, perfection worked in Him, and he was not distracted by the needs of inferiority or insecurity. Against the claiming crowd, He was not harsh but affable, saying to them that He needed to be elsewhere.

At the Lake of Gennesaret, later on, a crowd encircled Him and pressed on each other and on Him that they might for a moment have a part of Him. The crowd were not at their best, but they were what they were—like a thirsty, bustling herd that smelled the smell of water. Jesus knew the crowd would not give way under the refined manner of civility; therefore He pushed out into the water in Simeon's boat. Indeed, He could very well speak to them all along the shore, the water and the wind being a natural assist in the propagation of His voice.

After He was done, He called out to Simeon to set sail toward the deep and to throw out his net and other nets besides. Simeon confessed that he had toiled all night for nothing, that the nets were clean, that the Lord might not know the waters as the fishers did, but that he would toss a net out anyway. A gentle hand could not hold the net, because when it was cast out, numerous fish beyond the capacity of the net amassed as by a miracle. When Simeon saw all the fish, which were more than he could gain, he called out to another boat for help. And when Simeon saw all this, being suspicious of a miracle, he knelt down at Jesus' feet in guilt. What they had thought was natural, was no longer theirs to trust, and Simeon and his friends were bewildered and afraid. Then Jesus said to them, giving them a hint of how they ought to be, "Have no fear. Soon you will catch men instead of fish."

It happened in time, when He was at a certain place, that a disfigured man under the withering effects of leprosy took note of Him. The leprous man came up, feeling foul, and fell down upon his face, saying, "Lord, if You're willing, You can make me clean."

Immediately Jesus said, "I am willing." When He looked at the man, He stretched His prime hand out to the man, His compassion and His faith more daring than the sickness and its spread. Instantly, the man was to his best hopes healed, and all his body parts and his skin were to their best condition brought. In spite of years of slackened gait, he was up and running wild, being for his joy in a sort of feral mood, making game between his joy and feet.

All the healings of the Christ accrued for Him a name, inferred by the roaming crowds who thought Him unusual, who thought Him out-of-place. Even the Pharisees and the teachers of the law strayed into the mix that they might see if He was doing something devious.

One day some men brought in another man on a stretcher, a man who could not walk, and they tried for the man's sake to get close to Jesus and lay him nearby for a chance of notice. Purpose may do what languidness may not, and the ardent men reduced the roof of the house to something of a hole, that in spite of the thickness of the crowd they might get close. The intrusion of the descending man might offend a lesser man, but Jesus saw in all their labor faith, whereupon He said to the paralyzed man, "Your sins are forgiven."

Now the Pharisees and the scribes who were in the crowd muttered inwardly, "What is this thing that sounds like blasphemy, that He Himself surmises to take sins away?"

Knowing their thoughts, Jesus answered them, "Which is easier to remove, a sickness or a sin, because I know you deem them as equivalent. Therefore, watch Me now, that you may know who I am. Arise," He said to the man, "take up your bed and walk."

The uncertain Pharisees and scribes knew not how to applaud or denounce the progress of the matter, because the paralyzed man instantly got up, glorifying God.

Soon after, Jesus walked through the town. He noticed a tax collector in his booth. And Jesus, walking by with the seeming indifference of fortitude, said to the tax collector, "Follow Me."

Perhaps Levi (which was the name of the collector) knew that some moments in life came only once. Levi thought enough of this distinction and this call that he conclusively dropped his money and his booth and ran after Him—because Jesus did not stop to wait. Running thus, Levi came up and offered Him a meal.

A good degree of condemnation had gripped Levi, the penalty for dealing with the taxes, and he was ever unable on his own to reverse—even with his wealth—the numbered stares of blame each day by those from whom he took. It was this feeling that helped him stand up so quickly against his past. There was someone on his side, a respite—no, a redemptive glance—and for a moment he saw the other side of repentance, the secret side that says there is no guilt. Therefore, when he came to his home, he made a great feast for Jesus.

Nursed in the ways of the law and in the polluted lap of self-righteousness, the Pharisees increased against Jesus, saying to Him, "Why do you eat with sinners?"

Jesus told them of His distinction, that He had come across the way, holding sinners rather in His prospect, and that He spent His time as a physician would with the sick. Again the Pharisees, who connected their uprightness and pride with the weary ways of rigid works, inquired of Him, asking, "Why do Your disciples make no prayers or fastings like those of John or even those of the Pharisees?"

He said, "How can the friends of the Bridegroom fast when they are with Him during the time of His preparation? Nonetheless, there will come an occasion for them to fast and pray when He's taken away from them."

Jesus went on teaching, introducing them to a new disposition that they would not understand, saying to them, "One does not knit a piece of new garment on an old, because it might cause a tear. And imagine wine in the same light. No one puts new wine into old wineskins; they are incompatible, and the new wine will burst out, ruining the old wineskins."

On another Sabbath, Jesus walked through a grain field. His disciples walked alongside Him, and in the ease of the moment they began to pluck the heads of grain and eat. But the irksome Pharisees who were following them around came behind, accusing, "Why are you breaking the law? It's the Sabbath, and it's forbidden to do so."

Tradition always assumes the bad trait of an oppressor when it can no longer stand tall on its ossified legs. And Jesus, being aware of their intent and their traditions, wherein they exceeded but did not excel, answered them, "You've read so much, but have you not read of David, who took the showbread when he was hungry? I am the Son of Man, Lord of the Sabbath."

The Pharisees soon after began to see how they might reduce Him to a heretic. It followed later, on another Sabbath, that they sat watching Him, to make an index of His deeds. A man was there who had a withered hand. The Pharisees spied closely and hoped that the man might aid them to their end. Jesus knew how they thought, and He had the man with the withered hand stand up. Jesus then asked, "What is lawful on a Sabbath: to do good or evil, to save a life or to destroy a life?"

Having posed the question so, He looked around at them to see what they would answer; but the Pharisees looked blank, only staring back. To the man He said, "Stretch out your hand."

The Pharisees breathed out a short sigh, not of surprise, but something more of heated air, because they glanced upon the healed hand with rage.

Whatever facility Jesus had from the uncorrupted spirit within, He still required the occasional and pleasant solace where He would pray. One night He was on the mountain by Himself. To His Father, all His prayers felt right, felt clean, and they turned into reward. Next day, He called disciples to Himself, the twelve who would be for Him outstanding: Peter and his brother Andrew, James and John, Philip and Bartholomew, Matthew and Thomas, James, Simon called the Zealot, Judas the son of James, and Judas Iscariot who was to be the traitor. Having sanctioned the twelve, He came down lower from the mountain to a great and varied multitude—people not only from Jerusalem and Judea but from the seacoasts of Tyre and Sidon.

The people were all glad that between tradition and pain a hope was found, and it was a most awesome day. They came in waves around His light—some reeling, some limping, all stretching out their seeking arms that they might touch Him as they passed—because a voluntary power had begun to transfuse from Him as if in radiance, healing them all and delivering them all from unclean spirits.

He said to his disciples, "There is a hope and a kingdom for everyone, but especially for those who are hungry and those who weep, those whose sight is not veiled by the fabric of the fullness of pride. The stomach has contempt when it is full, and the heart says there is no need for a plough or seed or water for the branches of the tree. If you cannot in your only days stop to press into the better Life, then you might find yourself expended and your days amiss. If indeed you wish to be like the Most High, you need to be perfect. But you are unable. Should you not therefore believe in Me for the way? The heart by its own suggestion gloats that it needs no major teacher, but really, what peerless height can one achieve when one admires oneself? The bosom throws out many rows, many dim footpaths for the feet. If you find your will your master, find as well a master for your will. Everyone thinks they can see well, that they will by their private hope or silence or peculiar knowledge have a chance against the designs of fate. But what will happen if the blind lead the blind? They'll be at large with their best hopes, pressing eagerly into some dusty course, not knowing.

"And why do you never look at your brother as equal? It's because you've built yourself up high; yet your little structure is not marvelous, and the structure of the standing-stool upon which you stretch is made from thistles, not wood. How can you therefore say to your brother, 'Let me help you because I've found a speck in your eye, because surely it will hinder you in seeing things as well as I.' First look at your own eyesight and remove the plank that covers and flatters it, so that your relief might survive the blindness of your pride. A good tree can't grow remote from its good fruit; a good tree yields from its stores and in its seasons good fruit, and a bad tree in the same way the barren and the bad. You all have more need to come to Me to hear My sayings, and if you do them, you'll be like the heedful man who built his house upon a rock; his heart was deep and high, as he had taken steps on the eternal stair. And when the flood arrived and beat about for the sacking of the house, it could not even with its meanest wave have its offense, because the house was on a rock. There was another man who heard but didn't do My words; he had no care, and he built his house upon the sand. And his house had not its being long; the flood was quick, and there was no mercy from the sand."

Following His sayings, Jesus went into Capernaum, wishing to proclaim Himself there. His audiences consulted Him as something less than the promised and dawning light, yet they listened with interest and with something of awe. Their fixation or gaze was below the aim of redemption. Bemused, they followed Him that He might supply to their delight a titillation. The crowds, by and large, had their hearts in ironic dissonance, hinged and vacillated as to a fad of yet another transient and meteoric sage. Nonetheless there was the occasional person with better and lucid perception.

Here rose a certain centurion to the front; he was peculiar from the common people in that he was generous, despising nearby greed for the sake of another's comfort and giving much alms to the poorer Jews. The centurion's servant got sick, and according to the fruit of his good heart, he gave grave consideration to his servant and asked the elders of the Jews to seek out Jesus. For this reason, the elders came to Jesus with the plea, telling Him of the servant who was sick and the centurion who had gained a good standing among the Jews for his gifts. The elders might have thought their advantage was the backdrop of the good centurion, yet love has its own determination. Though pleading falls below the power of persuasion, God's moves are paved ahead of Him by some other, stranger agency. For whatever reason, when God senses faith, He has facility.

It pleased Jesus to turn aside, finding the permissible road toward the house of the centurion. The centurion saw Jesus coming on the road, and he felt he could not sanction in himself sufficient worthiness to endure the presence of the holy Man. Therefore, he sent some servants out to meet the Lord, to say to Him that there was no need to bring His likeness to the unbecoming house: "Say only on this occasion the word, and my servant will be healed, because I've likewise in my career authority that fetches the expected demands however I may wish; and when I tell this one to go there, he goes, or to do this, he does."

When Jesus heard this statement, He stopped and marveled at the man, saying aloud, "What great faith!"

Jesus went on, saying, "The servant will be well."

In that moment, faith and words opened their buds to bloom, and nature and the sickness capitulated to the force of the threads of the spirit. Immediately the servant was healed.

The next day, Jesus walked to Nain, and a crowd followed Him. As He reached the gates of Nain, a second smaller crowd passed by. The small group had little fever, their faces somber and cautious, and they walked on their way in thuds, the clomping gait of a funeral procession. They carried a dead man out, the only son of a widow. When the widow passed, the Lord saw her pale countenance and He said with compassion to her, "Don't weep anymore."

Then He spoke to the dead man. "Arise!"

The crowd saw as with one eye the young man up and alive, and they were at first mute as by the breathlessness of fear and then loud within a shout, giving glory to God for the miracle.

Meanwhile, the nefarious Herod could not equalize his insecurity with his state and pomp, and when an occasion allowed him to show his mercy, he showed instead his scorn, because John the Baptist had with a slight offended him. Herod had with condescension his own brother's wife taken for himself, and John the Baptist had exclaimed from the desert his view against the deed and the lusty Herod.

Narcissism always swells its fortress to the apex of the dippy clouds, that it might be good in the little soul's sight, that bad things might not sting so sore, that it might easily, with its bulwarks and its bricks, knock the lesser dangers down. It was therefore for Herod a paltry course to take, to put John the Baptist under arrest. Herod could only obtain relief by putting him to death, but he kept John alive, fearing the agitation of the people who perceived him as a prophet and a light. It came to pass, however, during a banquet for his friends, that Herod sat unmindful on his seat, sat soft and smiling at a dance—a dance by Herod's daughter—and his sensibility gave way to a mixture of delight and drunkenness. And when he had this stupor on him, he said to his daughter, "Ask away. Ask anything. What can I give you, up to half of my kingdom?"

The lively daughter could not help herself, and she leaned over to her mother, Herodias (Herod's brother's former wife). Herodias whispered in her daughter's ear, her face betraying a sneer. For her mother's sake, the daughter then said out loud, "I want John the Baptist's head!"

The heavy-footed words dared Herod and his vow, and he could not, across the faces of the nobles, surpass the fateful words by any means. Herod's honor and John's death were one, and were expressive when the dead man's head stunned the nobles on its silver plate.

One day, one of the Pharisees thought it curious to invite the Lord to eat with him. Now when Jesus was at the table, a woman, who was a sinner of repute, came walking up, shedding tears. She leaned herself down toward His feet and reached her hair to wash His feet and wipe her tears from them. Her actions were measured in love and gratitude, and no gift was thought too light or unfair. She had brought an alabaster flask of costly oil with which to bring her tears toward a fragrant end; she kissed His feet and poured the oil thereon.

The Pharisee who had invited Jesus sat across, watching the unexpected scene in silence, busy in a private moment of contempt. But Jesus said to him, "I have something to say to you. See what you can make of this. A certain moneylender had two debtors: one owed five hundred denarii and the other fifty. Neither could supply their amount because they were deficient. And when the moneylender saw their conditions, he forgave both of them all their debt. Which of the two will love him more?"

The Pharisee answered, "I suppose the one who was acquitted best."

Jesus answered, "You've judged correctly. And this woman here, who was under the obedience of sin and guilt, has acknowledged her love and righteousness in the language of her tears. It's true, therefore, that he who has been forgiven little, loves little."

Looking at the woman, Jesus said, "Your sins are forgiven, and your faith has saved you."

The people who sat at the table could not compute His latest words, saying to themselves, "How can He forgive sins?"

To them, sin ought rather to be exposed by the honest reflection of the Law and to be consulted and expunged by means of fanciful tries before their God. Since the bloody operations of the law only covered but did not remove the stains of sin, they wondered how there could be such things, or such a Man, that could have more effect than Moses and his scaping goats?

History records this woman as outstanding, while others left themselves useless in the crowd. While some people followed Him with excitement, their view no higher than their mood, others' desperation recommended zealous pursuit. There were some women who could no longer keep their comfort in the crowd, and they fought by faith, not fate, to come into His inner circle. Of note were Mary called Magdalene, out of whom came seven demons, Joanna, the wife of Chuza, Herod's steward, and many others; these helped Jesus lead His life, helped Him with whatever need suggested.

On another occasion, some days after, He taught the people again, speaking in parables. "A farmer went out to sow his seed. It was in this great spread that some seed fell to the side and were quickly trampled on, and the birds of the air came and did to them what they could. Other seed fell unhappy on a rocky soil, and when they had their little roots, they grew no more in height but withered for the dryness of the ground. Some others were scattered among the thickets and their thorns, and the seed and the thorns grew up together, but the former became burdened under the weight of the latter and were in time choked out. Still other seed fell into good soil and entered with all their state into a harvest, yielding a great crop."

His disciples afterward asked Him what the story meant. He answered, "The seed is the word of God. Those people who stand beside the road hear the word but find it not with faith; therefore the Devil comes and takes away the word, for he looks about for it. As for those whose hearts are like the rocky soil, they hear quite gladly and with faith. But in the inevitable time of temptation, they are relaxed and accept the fatigues of growth; therefore, in the terrible sight of a little struggle, they find the word no more. The ones who can carry themselves a little further in their faith are those who stand a little in the thickets and the thorns, but they stand not yet enough to survive the worries of the world or the indulgences of life. However, the seed in the good soil are reflective of the people whose good and honest hearts yield not conveniently to the windy turns of life and thought; they do instead press in, an iron in their gaze."

In those days, He was preaching all around. He was as the people in flesh and in breath, but He breathed a higher breath, some other wind within, and the people could not yet take in what was so free in Him. One day He got into a boat and said to His disciples, "Let's cross over the lake."

All was well at the launch of the boat, and Jesus went to the hull of the ship to sleep. A fierce gale picked up to smite the now tossing boat, yet Jesus slept in the comfort of peace. The disciples took His sleep as idleness, and when they for their fright and disarray could try nothing better—because the boat began to fill with water—they came to Him and cried, "Master, Master, wake up! Don't you care that we are about to drown?"

Jesus got up and looked at the wind and waves, and he must have seen them differently, must have seen them miscreated; therefore He rebuked them and they ceased. As for the disciples who had bowed before to the labor of the storm, they now bowed to Him within their hearts with fear, and they said to each other, "Who can this Man be?"

At length the boat arrived at the shores of the Gadarenes. A man quite shaken arrived there too: the madman of Gadarene, who had no saving in his own being. A demon had taken his beauty down, had wrung his soul all out. Indeed he ran about naked, being agitated by the operations of the demon. The poor man had been left to such things for years, eventually abandoned to his rabid reputation, this because the Gadarenes had failed in their cause to pacify him. At first they had tried with ambition and the associated hand of physical force for the sake of the possessed man. But when they could not command the demon to good behavior, the auxiliaries of chains and shackles and guards took the place of their earlier strains. The madness found fault with the iron, found them easy things to rip, and always in the end the man returned with impatience to the tombs, where he groped and moaned, day and night.

When this man saw Jesus arriving on the shore, he fell before Him and cried out, shouting loudly, "What do I have to do with you, Jesus, Son of the Most High God? I beg you, don't torment me!"

The demon was discharging in this way, because Jesus had commanded it to leave. Now the demon carried itself with much panic and gave up its name, which was Legion (because many demons had entered the man). The demons argued for their predicament with more than an ordinary intimation of fear; in fact they begged Him in the most severe screeching, asking Him not to command them into the abyss.

As far as the abyss, curiosity totters merely around the figure of that deep and infamous pit. Senses are too idle or unwilling to wake imagination to the awful height, or perhaps depth, of its reality. The clever or repulsed mind answers quickly, bargaining with the convenience of ignorance or suppression or even time, and suggests to the doubtful soul of no such things. Rather it falsely advises that the truth is in the average: Seek some good in between, it says; do not win too well in life; do not reach for far-off things that may take you off too far.

Now the demons, in their panic, resourcefully proposed that they might be sent into a herd of pigs that were feeding on a nearby hill. The lament of the demons betrayed their lack of authority, and it appeared they could not even obtain the pigs as hosts without permission. Therefore they said to Jesus, "Give us permission to go into the pigs."

Jesus allowed this. His heart had in it no strange dissonance, no mercy incited by the sorry pleas of the devils. If any pity, it was in the cause of the man, for whom He wanted swift relief. Besides, He perhaps thought that for the demons and the pit there was given a future time for retribution. However it worked, when the demons entered the pigs, the pigs took off with either the miscalculation of a frightened beast or the skillful direction of their new hosts, and they set a bolting course toward a cliff. The pigs got what they had not sought after, tumbling off into the sea. From the foam and waves and mist, half-rising, the demons rose naked to the air and then made their way to land, because they found offense in the water—and in flame as well—being excluded from all elements of comfort.

The pig-herders watched the scene with trepidation and then went baffled to the town to tell how the day was made peculiar. The whole town stuck with each other in the quest of curiosity, and when they came to Jesus and saw the madman clothed and well, they divided not to joy but rather to the unrighteous mood of fear or loss, having more care for the herd of pigs than for the heart that once had pain. This Jesus was for them not for salvation, but nearer to nuisance; therefore they asked Him to advocate Himself elsewhere.

The glad face of the liberated man had the best example of delight and gratitude, subjecting its shine to its Savior and pleading to walk with Him forever. But Jesus gave Him another charge, to go back into the heedless town and tell of the good that God had done. It was the herd of pigs that turned faith to fear, and apart from the light upon one glad man, there was a certain tragedy in the scene. However innocent in their determination, the people of the Gadarenes had done themselves and the visiting Light great wrong. They could not even marvel, to their own expense, knowing not the Wonder who had come and left. Meanwhile Jesus complied with their antagonism, as love would do, and returned across the lake. There again, on his arrival, a multitude was waiting for Him to come into their sight.

There on the shore was Jairus, a leader of a synagogue, who came up to Jesus with the spontaneous outpouring of a rambled plea, and that for his twelve-year-old daughter who was very sick. What else was the father to do but with all his might to ask and trust? How opposite was this man from the fluttering Gadarenes. Unlike them, Jairus was more severe, a sort of hunger within, and he had an open breast from which and to which great things could reach.

Jesus agreed to heal Jairus' daughter and took a course to his house. Jesus passed through the might of the pressing crowd, because in this throng, space and politeness were defied for advantage. In this seeming random bustle, a woman came from behind Jesus under the necessity of desperation, having had a flow of blood for many years and many cures that had cured her not. Then up close, when she had gained near enough to grab the hem of His robe, she grabbed the cloth and reached beyond to touch His power and her faith. And that which had long been for her a wound was healed at the very instant of her touch. Jesus perceived that power had flowed out from Him. He changed His step and stopped and looked around and asked aloud, "Who touched Me?"

Peter, who was perhaps growing rash against the throng, said back, "Lord, how can You ask this, because as You can see the people are pressing on you the whole time?"

Sincerity, one supposes, betrayed the woman and her touch, and when she saw she was stared upon with bidding insistence, she came trembling before the Lord, crying out the reason for the daring touch, saying that she had indeed taken hold of His hem and had been healed. Jesus answered her, saying, "Daughter, be happy, your faith has made you well."

While He was still speaking, something else instilled itself into the mix—bad news that made heaven's warmth seem intermittent and random in its pity. Someone from the synagogue had come and said, "Trouble the Teacher no more, because it's too late. The little girl has died."

But Jesus was not that sporadic; and He admonished Jairus to keep his faith, that the daughter would be made well. When He came to the house, the mourners were loud and screeching, and hope had dwindled also to its death. He sent them all out of the room, saying, "Don't cry. The little girl is not dead but asleep."

The mourners did not acquiesce to this advice, only that they began to privately snicker and mock Him for His discernment, for they had seen the daughter dead. He took her by the hand and said, "Little girl, get up."

Jairus had no better sight than when he saw his daughter rise, because her spirit returned into her body and she got up. And Jairus, with his little faith that worked, was astonished, and in his eyes was the turning of his tears.

Chapter 22

— ⊰ ✠ ⊱ —

Regardless of the devotion roused within the crowds through those years, Jesus warned his disciples and the people that the Son of Man was not admitted into this world to get His kingdom or His crown through the fervor of adulation. Instead, the Son of Man would obtain His height when the people saw Him in His sorrow, rejected by the priests and elders, receiving by mankind's hands an ironic death. But He would not share forever the deep of the earth; only three days and then He would rise up from bitter pain to power, the Seed sown low and deep to be forever settled like the sun.

He taught them other things as well, saying, "Mankind shouldn't function by their own strength, because their hearts have made-up dreams and little hopes like clouds dispossessed of wind. Better to feel an internal Wind that can change tired life to youth. Try not to save your own soul as you see it, collecting vainly like a crow some shining baubles for its scattered nest, baubles to which the imbecilic crow is happy to apply the false designations of sapphire, jasper, and chrysolite. Even if you could by your skill cast yourself so wide as to take over the entire world, wouldn't you have a part in death or judgment? All your heaps of gold, your heaps and heaps of things that are meant to defend you, will come to the ruin on that awful day that you dread, the day of your death.

"You may raise yourself by your own education, having polished the idea that you are not afraid of death, that there is no more after this, that you have had a good life as compared to the miserable masses. You may even have that outstanding worse thought, the awful veil and false thought, believing that your little bit of goodness will be to God or heaven a sufficient maneuver to enter into life eternal and bliss forevermore. Yet however artful you are to deceive yourself, you'll not escape the truth. Praise God then that you're not cast out to bear more than what you can, that you need not pray out loud and perfectly in the chance that your taxing investment may obtain you strength toward salvation. Indeed, the new covenant is here, and you need no longer grind against a sort of thwarting granite, pushing as it were with your weary hands against an inaccessible rock. Therefore, whatever narrow limits you may have suggested to yourself to obtain salvation, know that He grants you latitude in this way: that you should believe in Him and call on Him, and that alone."

Jesus was also teaching them, saying, "There are some here who will see the kingdom before they see their death."

It happened in consequence, about eight days after, that He took Peter, John, and James up on a mountain to pray. However stern the three disciples had meant to be there on the mountaintop, they could not keep their eyes open on account of the sleep that wandered in on them, the gentle heavy force of sleep that finds the pleasant places of the mind. So sleep found the three out, and meanwhile Jesus kept on praying. As He prayed, some sort of light began to shine, amending Him, as it were, and His clothes gave off the shine and dazzle of the sun's glory; but this was not a mere stray ray from the moon, nor did the sun glance in at night upon the Man. Instead it was His inner light that leaped as though outside its season to the range and reach of flesh. On this mountaintop, heaven sank and shone its window bright, making out of its glory and its light a promotion of its Lord. From heaven's side, where it is ever morning, stepped forth Moses and Elijah into the night. The occasion was for them to talk to Jesus about His death and resurrection, according to the plan of redemption.

When Peter woke from what he had of sleep, he saw the Lord shining—and Moses and Elijah. In Peter's bewilderment, somnolence not being an able guide, he muttered something forth, saying, "Lord, let's make some tents for You and Moses and Elijah, and we can all stay here."

As Peter was saying this, the air turned into a cloud, and the cloud floated as a little bit of mist might when it finds the center of a pond, when it becomes the object of a morning beam that seeks it out with its waking stream. In this way the cloud was singular, needing metaphors to describe its dazzle and its glory.

The Cloudmaker had spent this cloud not in vain, because He spoke from out of the cloud, saying, "This is My beloved Son. Listen to Him!"

The cloud dissipated, and the majestic event left no suggestion for response on the part of the befuddled disciples, who said nothing, applying only silence to their mystification and their fear.

Next morning, they all came down from the mountain. Yet again a multitude had gathered, and a man cried out to the Lord, "I beg you to look at my son, my only son, for a spirit takes hold of him and tosses him with convulsions this way and that. I asked Your disciples to cast the spirit out, but they couldn't, regardless of their attempts."

They brought the boy to Jesus; He rebuked the demon, and it launched out with shrieks and fits. The boy was cured that hour, and there was something glad and flushing in his face. The disciples had watched their own failure with curious disappointment, and they watched the Lord in amazement and asked in private why they could not cast the demon out.

Jesus answered them, "It's because you had wandered off from faith to the ruins of philosophy. When you debated with the scribes that morning, you became entwined with unbelief, believing that faith has a home in flesh or reason. In this example you have tasted the secret strength of unbelief. This kind of doubt is full of expectation; this kind of unbelief can only be cast out of you by prayer and fasting. You should therefore find a way for your little faith to survive your unbelief. Indeed, you need only a little bit of faith, comparable to a tiny mustard seed, and then you may say to this mountain, 'Be cast into the sea,' and it will be cast forth. But once grace comes, it will labor for you for faith, even My very own faith."

Through those years there was the constant effusion of marveling among the people and the disciples, yet Jesus did not take the appellations for pride. He resisted these temptations, the glory of the moment, the winged thought of relish that He knew would be lost in the very next gust. Privately He informed his disciples of the dissonance in the roar of the acclamations, of a space left for something awful: that the Son of Man was to be betrayed into the baneful hands of mankind. Yet the disciples could only obtain a curiosity from this divergent statement, as it was incompatible with the capable success of the moment. Being thus content with the conciliatory feeling, they made room for nothing else.

Under the surpassing effects of the roars and ruckus of the people, the twelve disciples were tempted and unable to repulse the beginnings of conceitedness. They, being fishermen, had left their sensibilities anchored to the little boats, and they began to make boasts and disputes as to whom among them were the greatest. Jesus, perceiving their hearts, took a little child and said, "Take this child for your example, because in his soul the buds of pride have not had leave enough to make his heart blush with this fault. You should be like him in innocence. Don't be like the world and their foremost. See how they like to lord it over each other, taking their servants' sighs as their puffs. But he who wants to be the first among you should be as one who serves."

Now Jesus was on His way to Jerusalem, and He sent messengers ahead to prepare His stays, wherever it might be. A particular village of the Samaritans refused to have Him in their inns and hearts, preferring instead the useless stagnation of sameness, and their rudeness formed their defense. James and John saw the offensive behavior of the town and said to Jesus, "Do you want us to call fire down from heaven and destroy the village like Elijah did?"

Jesus answered them, "You don't know from what spirit you are saying this; because I've not come to destroy mankind but to save them."

A seed clings not to itself but grows in death into another life. Indeed a forest strains within the shell, and when the shell dissolves into a grave, the seed begins anew into another growth. Clothed with flesh, the God-man Christ was like some sort of seed, and His reproduction resulted in time in a resurrected progeny. Meanwhile, at this point in history, the Seed had not yet been planted, and He went about working while it was day. He called and appointed seventy other disciples and sent them out by the strength of His authority to go about intercepting ordinary life with the teaching of a new kingdom, impressing and supporting the message by healing the sick and casting out devils. At length these seventy returned successful, and being surprised, they told Jesus, "Lord, even the demons obeyed us in Your name!"

Jesus answered them, "I saw Satan fall from heaven as a lightning bolt. Meanwhile, your happiness should not be in the subjection of these spirits but rather because your names are written in heaven."

A certain lawyer had moved himself, sidelong and conniving, near to the front of a particular crowd. He had in him the mix of lucid learning and the dimmer fog of thoughts that hung around protected pride. Therefore, he wished to impress Jesus with a decent question so that the decency might work enough to hide the test within. He asked Jesus, "Teacher, what should I do to get eternal life?"

Jesus answered, "What is written in the law? How do you read it?"

The lawyer answered, "You shall love the Lord your God with all your heart, with all your soul, with all your strength, with all your mind, and your neighbor as you love yourself."

Jesus said, "That's right. If you're able to do this, you'll live."

It appears the lawyer's mind had insensibly and imperceptibly taught himself that he could make an able work of loving God. The scales were for him easy, yet he idled on the latter point. Doubt stood too real within reality, and he wanted to justify himself. Therefore he asked Jesus, "Who then is my neighbor?"

Jesus told him a story. "A certain man went walking on the road from Jerusalem to Jericho, and as he walked, rogues came from the side and wounded him, and took from him, and left him for death. A little later and by chance, a priest came down the road, but when he saw the wounded man, he found a faster pace and took another way around. In the same way a Levite walked and came upon the man and passed by quickly, his mood and speed the same. A Samaritan came too, and when he saw the man, his compassion caused him not to guess his mood. He bandaged the man's wounds and took him to an inn, saying to the keeper of the inn, 'I'll pay for what he owes.' Which of these three was a neighbor to the man?"

Later on, Jesus went to a village, and a woman named Martha gave Him a reception. Now Martha was not content with mere accommodation, and she was busy with an exuberant effusion of care and hospitality. At the same time, Martha's sister, Mary, sat at Jesus' feet. Mary was unaware of the growing tempest in her sister's mind, a wind fanned by Martha herself. At length when Martha was worked up to a point of molten overflow, she said to Jesus, "Lord, don't You care that I have to do all the serving, while my sister is just sitting there but finds no fault in doing so? Tell her to come and help me!"

Jesus said, "Martha, Martha, you worry about too many things. Of all the many things in life, one thing is preferable. Mary has chosen the right part, and it won't be taken from her."

It was now many years since the fall of Adam, and mankind had yielded with passive accordance to life without the living God, being insensibly unaware of their dried-up souls, their sin making them like dried trees. And as they were—because of sin and fear and guilt—incompatible with the consecrated station of holiness and bliss, they grew upward to lesser lights and their roots grew to lesser waters, toward the sunken glories of the little comforts of the soul: prideful fancies, investments, and guises that might protect against the rot.

In this way mankind was full of loss, yet even in the barrenness that continuously settled in them, there was still a yearning not too far away, and it blew their thoughts as though by winds far-off toward a latent and timeless hope. Though time seemed to die in tombs and death, yet time seemed to live. Therefore, mankind did not take their graves for death, and another knowledge sprouted like a thirst to remind them of a lovely hope. Accordingly, mankind put a discontent in their days and habits: religious practices of some sort or another to satisfy the murmur of eternity within.

The people asked Jesus, "How shall we pray to God?"

He answered, "Pray in this way: 'Father, hallowed be Your name, Your kingdom come. Give us each day our daily bread. Forgive us our sins, for we ourselves also forgive everyone who is indebted to us. And lead us not into temptations.'"

This was the model prayer under the over-watching eyes of the Hebrew law, inasmuch as grace had not yet done away with all these troubles. But the mouth of grace prays better in this way, saying, "Father, hallowed be Your name; Your kingdom has come, our daily bread has come, our forgiveness has come, and our victory has come."

Meanwhile, the listening crowd discovered how prayer was not estimated through the convention of a haggling vendor. Instead, Jesus explained: "Suppose one of you goes to your friend's house at midnight, imposing at his door at that indiscreet time, and asks, 'Give me some bread, because I've someone at my house who arrived from a journey.' You hear your friend reply from inside the door, 'Please don't trouble me, because I'm already relaxed and my door is shut.' No, I tell you, he won't say that; rather he'll get up and give you the bread; but his giving won't be in the impulse of friendship. Indeed, it's because of his need to get rid of your persistence."

"And what you can take from this," explained Jesus, "is that your Father in heaven is not wearied out like this man. In fact, He sees your prayers not with the red and sleepy eyes of someone rolling slowly out of bed. So I say to you, ask and it will be given to you. Suppose again that one of you has a child who asks unassuming for some fish to eat. Will you in the moment of your child's expectation give something contemptible like a snake? If you who are innately evil know how to give good gifts to your children, how much more will your Father in heaven supply to you what you request—yes, even the Holy Spirit."

Once Jesus cast out another demon, and there were some people who were not impressed by His power, believing it was something darker from the occult, from the power of Beelzebub, the ruler of the demons. He knew their censured thoughts and said to them, "I cast out demons by the finger of God, therefore the kingdom of God is here. When a strong man is at home and attached to his palace, he sets around guards and whatever bulwarks are required for the protection of his precious goods. Now, when a stronger man comes upon him, he overthrows him and takes him down toward no armor and takes the spoil that fell around his tramplings.

"When an unclean spirit leaves the chambers of its host, it is diverted by its fretting through dry places where it means to find its rest. After a while, when it can't come to that advantage, it reminds itself of its past hold, saying, 'I'll return to the dwelling from which I came.' It comes and finds the old soul swept and clean, with things laid open and in order. For whatever motive, it goes and finds seven other spirits more wicked than itself and says to them, 'There sits my host all empty and in order. Let us enter him and make him worse; he won't give us much in argument.'"

Once there was an instance where Jesus was to dine with the Pharisees. It must be known that the Pharisees valued ritualistic virtue and cleanliness at the expenditure of actual morality. When Jesus sat down to eat, the Pharisees found it marvelous, and their inward thoughts curled up because they saw Him seated without a wash. Rules and rituals make brave the souls who can obey them, as they have by these deeds sundered themselves from perfect liberty. The human fragrance has left, and there is only left the reek of a judicial flame and smoke. Genuineness has long from the foul smoke fled, and conscience has been pruned from the weeping tree of mercy.

In such work-oriented minds, there are instead plantings in places without shade, that they might find at last the dry and castigating stick within its wood. Guilt mixes poorly with the heart but mingles well within the ready fluids of the mind. The mind can muscle out the bitter toxin; it quarantines it for the benefit of a constraining peace—to the detriment of liberty. Guilt insensibly suggests condemnation, a cruel species of emotion. The mind and heart collude, being in this conspiracy implacable to any attempts of denial. Therefore the heart is forced inevitably to either the habits of timidity and fear or to the vice of scorching the conscience—or last, to the introduction of an artificial and cultivated righteousness, amended and enlarged enough to be a covering.

And when the Pharisees stared at Him, He answered, "You Pharisees know too well the outside of the cup; it is for you the whole. Therefore you look with indifference toward the inside of it. Yes, it is darkened in the eyeless places of your heart so that you might not see it when it shines by chance toward your rigid conscience. Certainly, because your hearts are full of wickedness, you prefer the shining polish of the labor of self-righteousness over incessant guilt, and you prefer the bright glare of your public prayers over the dusk of private, humble prayer. You feel good when you subdue unrighteousness with an aspiring deed, because you are—with all your limbs but not your heart—busy with your tithes, giving mint and rue and all kinds of herbs. These things you should do while not passing love and justice by."

A lawyer who was sitting there too introduced himself in the train of slights, saying to Jesus, "Teacher, by saying these things, you are offending us as well."

Jesus answered, "Woe to you, lawyers of the Law. You listen not for the moans when you load up burdens on the people. You see your stake in them and feel good when they groan unfairly under all your rules. Indeed, as you go over your good laws, you do not lift a finger to help. You find your bravery behind the high fence of the law, being satisfied in full and able to decline the imploring voice of mercy and humanity. Self-appointed lords of history, you build monuments to the past prophets and crown their lives with your small life and your meditative thought, even as your very fathers took part in killing them. You might not have lived yourselves within your fathers' bloody scenes, yet all the blood from Abel to Zechariah will be required of you."

Afterward, Jesus spoke to the crowds, saying, "The grounds of a certain rich man produced much crop, and the rich man thought to himself what to do with it all. 'I'll pull down my barns and build bigger ones and store all my goods and all my crops. I'll say to my soul, "Soul, all my barns are completely full, and need no longer makes demands; therefore, eat and drink, and become used to the habits of ease."' But God said to him, 'Fool, this night your soul will be required of you. How can you defend yourself, and what will be the purpose of your wealth?'

"Consider the lilies, how they grow. They have a glory like the glory of God, yet they don't toil or spin. If God so clothes the plants that are soon shrunk and lost, how much more will He clothe you? When doubt is strong, or fear, faith won't give God a chance to change your wind-worn life or reach your far-off dreams that are so dear to you. But seek first the kingdom and His righteousness, and all these things will be added to you. And don't be afraid. It is His good pleasure to give you the kingdom.

"Don't be like the nations who hold their money with the severity of greed and fear, but rather, when you have obtained the kingdom and the righteousness, let your wealth be stored in heaven where it's not susceptible to the approach of the thief or destroyed by means of the moth. Indeed, your heart isn't a static station; it courses like a flood toward the sight of its own treasure, because where you treasure is, there your heart is also.

"Be better than a servant who gives back only what is directly observed, that you might be girded and awake, and remain with your lamp keen at the door, waiting for the master to return from his wedding. If he comes at night, he'll glance at you with the favor that crowns faithfulness; even more than favor, he'll answer his delight in you by girding himself as a servant to serve and seat you at his exalted table. In this way, you will do the Son of Man much wrong if you're conquered by the sleeping spirit of this age. Be instead at your mightiest, conceding to no indulging latitude during the last dark hours of the night, because for sure the Son of Man is coming at an hour you don't expect."

It happened in those days, or it was rumored, that Pilate had done a deed compatible with a most singular insult, or at least a cruelty, toward a group of Galileans for whom he had reserved his most spurned estimations, being satisfied to mix their blood with their own sacrifices.

When Jesus heard of this, He said to the people, "Do you suppose these Galileans had by greater sin this greater trouble? But I say to you, though the rod of sin is cruel and always follows after its delinquent, it follows sometimes with a patient crossing, a league behind its mark. Urged by the perceived ranking order of a sinner's sin, you judge some to be on sufficient ground to deserve an accidental circumstance, while others, by their better life, you deem far-off from ruin. In truth, the end of your lives is not constrained nor granted sympathy by this dichotomy. I tell you this: unless you repent, you'll all perish. Think about those eighteen on whom the tower in Siloam fell. Did sin's spear make the strike? I tell you again: unless you repent you'll all perish."

One Sabbath, Jesus was teaching in a synagogue, as was the habit of His steady manner. A woman was there, bent over in her soul, and the nerve that made her stand upright was impaired as though by the slights of life, or the dominion of a spirit of infirmity which had attached itself onto her spine. One could not overlook her, even though decency might constrain one to avert the eyes, because she had grown into a caricature, being entirely bent over in her spine—a sorry specimen that called up deepest sympathy. Upon the sight of this, Jesus called her instantly and said, "Woman, you are loosed from your illness."

One knows not which shot up erect first—her heart in joy which lifted itself unconfined toward the peaks of gratitude, or her brittled bones that, in duty to the healing and her joy, moved within the sprightly form of youth. The ruler of the synagogue did not find it in his narrow heart to kindly share the mirth, for the force of law had made for him no space that high. Rather, it placed him prone behind the bulk of grim pertinacity. From there he struck out, saying to Jesus, "There are six days for men to work, come back and heal on them, not on the Sabbath."

The Lord answered, "Hypocrite! With respect to your ox or donkey, don't each of you loose it from the stall and lead it toward water—even on a Sabbath? Ought not this woman, a daughter of Abraham, be loosed upon the Sabbath?"

When His adversaries heard this, silence was the shade that hid them from the prickly exposé, but the multitudes rejoiced in the glorious things that did so much for them.

Now Jesus was meant to be sown, but before He reached Jerusalem, He went journeying through many dusty paths for mankind's sake, teaching and healing with the sentiments of compassion. As for the feet of God that once walked upon the airy zones of gold, they walked at this time in history upon the grounds of earth, swerving not their tread as though the ground might be an awful lesser thing. He had given up the life above with the stars to offer by His new, low degree an aid for mankind's fate. Indeed He saw the dust as soil, and soil not less than the harvest. Though He might be sown, weak and natural, in the apparent emptiness of death and flesh, He would rise with every strength in spirit.

On His way to Jerusalem, someone asked Him, "Are there many saved?"

He returned, saying, "Strive now and thirst, that you may move yourself toward the open door. Solicit yourself, that you find not the negligence that will surely make you sad when you straighten yourself out too late to go through the open door, discovering in perpetual pain that it is forever locked. Go to that sure door. Intercept your own way there with a sensibility, and when you find it, don't glance sideways, because neither pity nor even all of love nor another pretended door will admit you once it's shut. When once the Master of the house has gotten up and shut the door, and you come up with indifference or shock, and knock on the door, He'll answer you, saying, 'I don't know where you are from.' And then you will begin to say, 'Why, Lord? Were we ever cold to you? We even heard you in the streets.' But the Master will say, 'You were never warm to Me; your closed heart closed the door for you.'"

One day a man who could no longer resign his wonder of the things he saw of Jesus to mere swellings in his chest, exclaimed as though involuntarily to the Lord, "Blessed is the one who will dine in the kingdom of God!"

The Lord gave an answer with the facility of a parable. "A certain man prepared a joyous feast, and he said to his servant, 'Go out and call in those invited to my joy. The work and food are now all done.' The servant went out but was in silence shocked, because those invited made wide excuses not to come. One said, 'If only I had expected this some other time, because, you see, I'm just now on my way to view the land I've bought.' And another said, 'I know nothing more pleasant than the present feast; however, I'm standing in disparity, having just married, and owing therefore care to my wife.' Still another said, 'It's not that I've been affected by indifference, but it's important that I should look after my cattle, because I've bought some just now—five yoke of them that are to be tested out.'

"When the master heard this, and knew his hopes were improperly respected, he was angry. The reproach did not fix in him the soft look of defeat. Instead, he called his servant and said, 'Go out quickly into the streets of the city and look for clues of those in need. Find the poor, the maimed, the lame, and the blind, and bring them in as one who reaps a willing yield.' The servant did that and returned, saying, 'Master, many came, yet there's room for even more.' And the master said, 'Let my invitation try out elsewhere. Look for those who might have lost themselves in the highways and the hedges, and ask them, with much urging, to come to the feast and have their fill and pleasure.'"

Jesus spoke another parable to them, saying, "What shepherd won't, in his concern, leave his flock of sheep behind and go out searching that he might discover a single lost one? His hope and sympathy take him out on his errand, and his face changes not until it finds the object of its passion. When found, the shepherd lays the sheep on his shoulders and comes home, looking to give his friends the good news. In this way, joy that has long left rises up in heaven over one sinner who returns.

"And again, a certain man had two sons, the younger of which became restless. He regarded something above the comforts of home. In time his fancies inferred upon his reason the idea of a better life, and he petitioned his father for his portion of inheritance. On receiving this, he took a zealous course out in the world, going to a far-off country and spending his money to the degree of every immediate pleasure and every dream. But poverty soon replaced his delights with the peril of starvation, because he had come near to this by his foolish spending and by the coinciding and pernicious effects of a famine. And he asked himself what he should do. By the persuasion of hunger, he joined himself as a slave to another man, that it might supply to his survival. Hopeless thoughts came to him in the field, because it was by means of feeding pigs that he could obtain some sustenance. He felt offended to look at the pigs and degraded to stare at the pods they ate. Hunger would not spare his dignity nor grace his decency, and he felt compelled to take some of the pods and eat, but his master did not let him do even that. In a fervent moment, he came to himself, thinking of his father—and his father's servants, who were better off than he. 'I'll get up and go back to my father and cry to him that I've sinned and that I'm not his son but would be a servant to him.'

"Meanwhile, time had not put to sleep the heart of his father, who had each night lain awake, worried, and each day gazed dreamlike at the road that he might tell himself of hope. Then one day, when the father saw his son far off, he had to look again to mark reality, and he couldn't help the effect of love that hurried him along toward his son. When he came to his son, he fell on his neck and kissed him. The son, however, couldn't forget the writhing of his shame, and he cried out, 'Father, I've sinned and am not worthy as a son.' But for the father there was no pause, only joy, and he called out to his servants to bring a splendid robe, sandals, and a ring, and to prepare the fattened calf for a feast, because, he said, 'My son was dead and is alive again. He was lost and is now found!'

"Now the older brother was in the field, and when he became aware of the fragrant happiness in the house, he made the whole thing hard and bitter, saying to his father, 'You've never been this good to me. You consider my brother with a feast, while you've not given me even a goat. And look, he searched out the harlots but wasn't in the least troubled by his lack of integrity.' His father answered, saying, 'My son, you've set yourself at a lower level than you are. You've always been with me. Why have you never seen that all I have is yours? I can't help but bring your brother as near as you, because he was lost and is now found.'"

Jesus went on, saying, "There was a certain rich man who laid upon his wealth; indeed there wasn't much between his silver and his soul. The rich man gratified himself with cloth in purple and fine linen, and he confessed himself perniciously as something almost made of gold. At his gate a certain beggar sat. Feeble Lazarus sat there, ignored, and received only silence when he pressed his face in hunger to the gate that the writhing of his face might mark for him a little mercy or a morsel from the table of the rich. In the rich man's sight, there was no regard to take himself to the comfort of the poor. Rather he took himself to the reproach of sin, being far lost in selfishness.

"In time Lazarus died and was carried by angels to Abraham's bosom, and the rich man died and was buried. The force of Hades got the rich man and his lot and caused the rich man to cry out in agony and objection. And he lifted his eyes and saw Abraham far-off and Lazarus in his bosom and in rest. 'Father Abraham,' the rich man cried, 'have mercy on me and ask Lazarus to dull my pain with a drop of water, because my lips are in this parched place dry.' Abraham answered, 'You didn't help Lazarus when you could, and you had no mercy when it could have furthered him and you. Besides this, it's not allowed for Lazarus to come over, because there is a gulf as large as all your life between us and you, and we can't cross over it.'

"Common words didn't suffice, and the rich man let loose into a plea, saying, 'I beg you then that you'll send Lazarus to my father's house. I have five brothers who are like me. Let Lazarus do well and go to them and tell them of this place of wretched torment, because they think it's scarcely possible.' Abraham answered, 'They have Moses and the prophets, their patient informants of the things of life and death.' But the rich man said, 'No, father Abraham, you don't understand. If a man is raised from the dead and goes about telling the truth of this hell, then my brothers definitely will believe.' Abraham returned, 'If your brothers don't listen to Moses and the prophets, they won't listen even to a resurrected man.'"

About that time in history, the people were full of curiosity about the end of time, and they put it to Jesus that they might settle their attention on something precise. He told them that the kingdom would not come in forms that eyes or hands could touch or take; rather it would come without observation, being internal. Nonetheless, there would be a Day for the Son of Man in which it would be proper to settle many things, and dread would fall as when lightning falls out of the sky. But first the Seed of Man must take His part in grief and be rejected by this generation.

Jesus predicted that prior to the end of days it would be as in the days of Noah. Whether the analogy referred to the carelessness and violence that stoked those days or to the miscreations who had been of old is unknown. As far as the hybrids, or Nephilim, they had appeared by means of the angels who had had intercourse with the daughters of men—angels who had taken their own domain with contempt, crossing over, despising the risk of their certain curse for the chance to mix with flesh.

In that far-off time, the unhappy offspring, the Nephilim or giants, discovered the compliments of their strength and stature, and they proceeded to employ themselves in the same way as their celestial fathers, teaching and taking on strange flesh. And being set on fire by a curse, they had the flames of lust that reached for them the wives they wished. As no little man could stop them easily, and as they burned so much within, they took to devouring, consuming without conscientious fear, even each other. Indeed, for them it was and will always be about lust and blood.

Beyond these awful instincts, their father, Satan, meant for them to reach toward the ruin of God's promised plan and to create disaster in the seeds of men and bad hopes for a pure lineage. By them he would, with the faintest of intimations, make an introduction of his antichrist, a conductor who would with apparent respect bring together the irruptions of society under the pleasures of a one-man rule, a Nimrod of sorts who would swell up in pride and action against the only God. It might be, therefore, when mankind takes the hybrids for their compliment and shares in their sentiments for sin, that a return in likeness to the times of Noah shall recur, and with it a great stirring for the Day.

Jesus also told them this parable, saying, "A certain man planted a vineyard and leased it out for a time to others. The man planned to recover the vineyard on his way back from a long journey. At the appointed time, he returned and sent out one of his servants to find an account of the fruit and to return with some of it. But the vinedressers informed the servant otherwise, and in bitter mood beat him down and endured him not at all. A second servant was sent to make enquiry, and again the vinedressers set him up badly and mistreated him with shame. A third was sent, and this time the vinedressers had had enough, wounding the servant to make the owner sure of their disagreement. At length the owner said to himself, 'What should I do? I'll send my beloved son. It's likely they will respect him.' When the vinedressers saw the son, they said among themselves, 'Chance takes its turn to us; what has the owner when he doesn't have his heir? Let's avail ourselves and kill him and usurp this place for us.' So they took him and killed him. When the owner found out, he was in wrath, and he went out and destroyed the vinedressers and gave the vineyard to others."

The crowd heard this parable, and they were sorry for the heir and for his end, and said, "May something like that never happen in real life."

Jesus answered, using the Scripture He had reserved for this: "What then is this saying all about, that 'The stone which the builders rejected has become the cornerstone?'"

The scribes and chief priests, who had heard the parable as well, arrived better at the meaning, understanding that its motive was told against them. Hate for strength and murder for device, so enlarged the scribes and priests, and they began to plot that very hour.

It was about three years now since Jesus had begun teaching the people. One night around that time, Jesus went to the Mount of Olives to pray. His disciples followed Him. About a stone's throw away from them, He knelt, saying, "Father, if it's Your will, take this cup away, should there be another way; nevertheless, not My will but Yours be done."

He prayed as a strong man in a strong fight. To take His part upon the cross was not the reason for His agony. The cross was not the reason for His sweat that had begun in water from His porous skin and ended by force of sheer tenacity to bleed its water out in blood. Rather, the reason for this fight was for the sake of love. The cross was joy for mankind's sake, but love would be unfit and would not save the unity of God. Love could not pass the imperious straits where and when the Son of God must die and the Father must take His love away. Because it would be in the moment of God's wrath, when the Son was shaken for the sake of sin, that the Scripture would be fulfilled by the Father's saying: "In a brief moment, I couldn't stand You and couldn't look on You whom I've stripped of life. You who were always with Me, tender and in love, now become distinctly gross, full of the disorder of mankind, imputed with its sickness and sin and loaded up with awfulness—so much so that I need to look away and to look on You as an opponent and strike You with My awful strike. But surely I'll heal You back and bring Your feeling back, when I let You see again with Your loving face My open face."

This was the extent of the struggle of the Son of Man, but an angel appeared in the garden and gave Him strength.

An open soul no doubt has in its ways some spice, and when in agony its essence cannot help but give out its breath in a scent; and round Him was most surely something sweet, though the sweetness of grief. Yet another smell was there that night, some other odor that was led on by a motley crowd of guards and priests—and Judas Iscariot hulking in their huddling midst. Darkness could not hide, nor could the treated smile on Judas' face, the wicked plan of force and betrayal. Now Judas had before entered upon this duplicitous design, having with regard to greed gone to the chief priests and arrived at the deal for betrayal for thirty pieces of silver. The deal was as cold as the method, because he would have his sign in love—that the one he kissed would be the one to take.

The crowd came upon Jesus, and Judas stepped out in that way, aiming the plotted kiss on the cheek of God. And Jesus said, "Judas, are you betraying the Son of Man with a kiss?"

His disciples saw that this was not the innocence of love, and realizing what was about to take place, they asked, "Lord, should we strike with the sword?"

Peter, without consideration or patience, took his sword impulsively and lashed out, perhaps not being very sure how or whom to stab, and chopped off the ear of the high priest's servant, who was also in the crowd.

Not willing to oppose or frustrate the plan of God, and with the care and love that were always in His notice, Jesus intervened, saying, "Hold your swords!"

In saying this, He touched the wounded servant's head and healed his ear. One can unlikely draw out the troubled feeling in that servant's mind, when he had beforehand set Jesus as a sort of rogue but now learned the generosity of love.

At any rate, in this way they arrested Jesus. Meanwhile, his disciples scattered. Jesus was resolute, having seen from afar the things that were now close, that He as God and man would take the hits that were meant for man. They led Him to the high priest's house and kept Him overnight. They mocked Him and beat Him and were devious, being led on by the sudden and pleasing effects of their apparent muscle. As these captors had no learned sensibilities that might have reserved some decency, and as they discovered gleefully that they could get away with the stirring of their sadism, they provided for themselves much sport, blindfolding Jesus and hitting Him, saying, "Prophesy for us! Who is the one striking you?"

The next morning, the elders of the people tried their hands and their pleasures at a council of the scribes and chief priests, leading Jesus in their grim midst. The council's strong emotions did not break in at the start, as formality restrained the outbreak of an early animation. They asked Jesus, "Are you the Messiah? Tell us if you believe so."

Jesus answered, "Will you crown Me if I answer yes, or will you let Me go if I answer no? Neither your denial nor your praise has form enough to matter, because hereafter and for sure, the Son of Man will sit at the right hand of the power of God."

They asked, "Are you then the Messiah, the Son of God?"

Jesus said, "Yes, I am."

The council, when they heard this, kept their glee inside, showing only on their faces the lesser show, the solemnness of seriousness.

"What more do we need? We've heard it from His own mouth."

They all rose and took Him to Pilate and began to accuse Him of many things in the strongest terms, that they might encourage the studious Pilate to settle on their side. The mind of Pilate, which had long been used to the elevations of his post, had enough distance by that height not to succumb at first to the charges brought by religious hate.

"I find no fault in this Man," Pilate said.

The roused council pressed on and would have hissed if they could have had their way with such a sound. Invoking the land of Galilee, the council aimed to compel Pilate to their cause. When Pilate discovered that Jesus was from Galilee, he had facility to impose the problem on Herod, who had jurisdiction over that area.

Herod took Jesus gladly, because his curiosity had always wished to meet Him that he might see a miracle. Herod appeared therefore as an eager inquisitor, asking many questions of Jesus that he might provoke a miracle by this means. When this demand and its perseveration were neglected by Jesus, Herod changed his mind and thought of Jesus as one might think of a pretender. The gentleness of curiosity and the patience of hope were soon gone from Herod. A flightiness set in, which, unashamed and in need of titillation and humor, began to draw out the meaner parts of his heart. Herod and his men of war began then to treat Jesus with contempt, arraying Him subsequently for display in a royal robe. Boredom, for whatever reason, is always there to defend against an endless thing, and this moderating thought at length intervened to turn the sweet pleasure of abuse into the sourness of labor. Off they sent Him back to Pilate, with Herod saying, "I saw not much of any crime."

That day, Herod and Pilate became friends, though before they had been at odds. Back at Pilate's place, the priests and scribes and the people were recalled. Pilate meant to use the occasion to set Jesus free, and he assumed that a flogging of the Man would have in it sufficiency to calm the zeal of the crowd. But zeal once lit with agitation has in mind far more, something more palpable that resists easy dissipation. They cried out, "Away with Him! Release for us Barabbas!"

It was the custom at this time of year to release some prisoner—an act employed as a measure of goodwill toward the people. Barabbas was a notorious prisoner, having inlaid his name with that of a murderer, being the leader of a violent sect. And when the priests and the crowd saw that Pilate had conceived to free Jesus, they became even more actuated with the barbarity of unrestrained emotion, having bound their will to the soul of the crowd, which was now as something of a machine that had lost the finer motions of man. Being bound in this way, they shouted, "Crucify Him! Crucify Him!"

Pilate had hoped for a lesser occasion, but when he saw the crowd was without reservation, and fearing a riot, he gave Jesus up to be crucified, and he let Barabbas go.

Outside the city, to a place called Calvary, Jesus was led and crucified. God's very eyes, and those of the angels, saw the wrath of the crowd, and saw the wrath of God, which He poured out, even before the foundation of the world, on the tender fleshy body of the Son of God. The wrath of God put in all the nails and raised Him up upon the cross and pressed Him to His death and to the grave. The crowds too tried their eyes at the awful sight, and some were intercepted by a shock, a darkness, and a quake—while some demeaned the event to the pleasure of indifference.

There was another group who stood there unconverted, who thought of themselves as useful instruments in the killing of God. They had come—some walking, some flying from the corners of the earth and from the lower planes of the air—as had Satan himself, chief in their midst, to save himself and his demon-peers from the Seed of Eve, who was meant to come upon the earth one day and make the expected crush on the head of the snake. Now Satan had long thought to try his murder in this way, and he even marveled that he could get away with his bruising.

Three times before, Satan had assumed to lift his sword against the Son. The first occasion came through the might of Herod, who had meant to defend his own crown by killing the newborns of Bethlehem. But God had defied the bloody attempt when He had sent an angel and the Child away by night.

The second time, that awful felon had supposed to murder Him through deception, when he reached out to Scripture to expand his scheme, saying to Jesus, "See, it says that the angels shall deliver you, that you will take no wound; therefore, then, it is your right to proof their saving hands by jumping down from the temple roof."

The third attempt was conceived by Satan through the aid of the hapless people of Nazareth, who were divided toward murder in a moment of derision, when they took Jesus by force, their enthusiasm for a cliff. In all these, Satan failed. There was always an escape and an impediment. And when Judas was well-formed for possession, Satan entered him to try his hand again. He treated Judas as the betrayer, and upon this success, he admitted Jesus into the eager hands of the priests and scribes.

Around the slopes of Golgotha, Satan had his armies grouped, because he had thought for sure that God would not acquiesce to having His Son so slain. The gleeful Satan could not understand why God had left His angel armies impotent, to behold only with stern face the death that moved upon the Son.

When Jesus was on the cross, He prayed, saying, "Father, forgive the people, because they don't know what they've done."

At length, Jesus perceived that He was nearing the end, and He cried out with a loud voice, "Father, into Your hands I give My spirit." Then He breathed His last.

On the first day of the week, Mary Magdalene, Joanna, Mary, the mother of James, and other women came to Jesus' tomb because they had in the struggles of their grief brought spices to be used for the benefit of the dead. The tomb was found open and empty. They were perplexed, not knowing if another hard thing had fallen on them. Suddenly two angels appeared to them. The women were insensibly afraid and bowed their heads to the face of the light.

The angels said, "Why do you seek the living among the tombs? He has risen! Remember then how Jesus had spoken of His time, that the Son of Man would be crucified but on the third day would rise again."

Afterward, the startled women hurried to the disciples and told them what had happened. The disciples could not handle the sudden change; their disarray was unable to moderate the strange story of the women. Peter at length got up and ran toward the tomb, and seeing it empty, he returned and remembered what the Lord had foretold, and he began to marvel.

Some days afterward, the disciples got together, their surprise and their talking supported by stories of His appearances all over the town. Still, their notion of His resurrection struggled with fortitude, when suddenly their minds had the occasion to muse no longer with hollow words of hearsay because, in their midst, Jesus Himself appeared in the room.

He said to them, "Peace to you."

The actual end of the disciples' minds was not that of peace but of a kind of fright that stuns the mind, and one supposes that if they had not been in a room with walls, which supplied something of a confinement, they would have run away. This was because they supposed Him to be a ghost. He said to them, "Why are you frightened? Look, it's Me. Handle Me for yourself and see, because a spirit doesn't have flesh and bones as you see Me have."

Yet the disciples' minds did not find much relief from this encouragement; fear and faith had met far too quickly. At length and through the serenity of a few minutes, they all finally came to their joy. Jesus spoke again, saying, "Remember how I told you of the Scriptures, that they were written of Me, that from the beginning to the end it was written and necessary for the Christ to suffer, to be crucified, and to be raised for the sake of mankind for the remission of their sins. Now you are witnesses of this. Go and tell this news to all mankind."

When the disciples heard these things and understood, they attached their hearts to Him, and they needed no encouragement as He led them outside as far as Bethany, where He blessed them and was carried up into heaven.

The disciples returned to Jerusalem, their hearts in a gleam, where they waited for something called the Promise of the Father, which was the Holy Spirit, who would endow them with some sort of power. It was the Day of Pentecost, and they were gathered in a room, the fruit of their happiness causing them to sing and pray in quiet zeal and easy union. Suddenly there was a noise from heaven, the sound like the gusty flight of wind when it rushes here and there. The sound filled the room, and from the sound appeared something to be estimated as a flying fire, which was dispersed or divided into lean flames, each upon a person's head, where it sat and grew. In this way they were shown the Holy Spirit, and in this way they were filled of Him; and their own spirits acknowledged this amendment in the terms of a new language and other tongues, as the Spirit helped them express.

In Jerusalem at that time, there were many devout people, specimens of that human thirst for God. They had heard the strange noise, and a great crowd came together to discover a plausible conclusion. These zealots were more than ordinarily curious about the noises, because they had heard the disciples speak in a remarkable strain—in the languages of the Parthians and the Medes, of Asia and of Egypt, and so on. They were perplexed, as they knew the disciples to be ordinary Galileans who now spoke so vividly of the marvels of God in turns and in eloquence in this language and that. But some others around had no willing interest in mind, and they said this was the rowdy course of drunkenness.

The pert accusation, like all slander, had no shell of confinement, and from its gaping cave came its vapor to the ears of Peter, who stood up and said, "We aren't drunk, as you suppose. Why, it's only the morning still, at any event."

Peter went on, saying, "I'll refer you to the prophet Joel, who prophesied that God would pour out His Spirit on all flesh and that they would all prophesy. This is the change of times. Remember Jesus of Nazareth, with whom you all are familiar, as He once held your attention by His miracles—and as you yourselves have handled Him by force and hate when you took Him to His crucifixion. Nonetheless, He's not laid as low as you'd intended, because God, in His purpose and foreknowledge, had made this allowance and has raised Him up, having severed death from Him because it was not possible for death to hold Him. David says this same thing when he prophesied of Christ, saying, 'You won't leave Me in Hades, nor will You let Your holy one see decay.' And David said again, prophesying of the future, 'The LORD said to my Lord, "Sit at My right hand, until I put your enemies beneath You."'"

These words of Peter did not miss their marks, and when the crowd heard them and became sensible of the Scriptures, they were taken by their own anguish, asking, "What should we do?"

Peter answered, "God has made a way that takes you from the faults of man and from the perversion of this generation. If you were looking for the truth, refer your hearts to this new way. Let everyone be baptized, that you might by this action signal the remission of your sins, and receive the gift of the Holy Spirit; because from now on, it's not hard for you to be in liberty, nor is it necessary to use your ordinary strains and labor to make Him be pleased with you."

Faith worked here with much agility, and three thousand of the crowd were saved that day. In the course of those immediate days, many souls were added to this first and little church.

One might think the wild fragrance of a new theology to be short-lived, compressed as a season between the apathy of the old and the dim forecast of an uncertain future. Yet though squeezed, the little church endured. In fact, the movement had for its foundation more than good news, more than the lure of novelty; it was led on by many miracles and signs through the hands of the apostles.

In one such instance, Peter and John were walking up to the temple to pray, and they came on a lame man who had enlarged himself there at the entrance, being pitiful and asking for alms. Peter said to him, "Look at us."

When he did, Peter healed him. The man was elated and tried the powers of his legs through the means of his joy, and he leaped and walked and then leaped again.

Meanwhile, the captain of the temple, the priests, and the Sadducees had gathered around to find out about the affecting occasion. They heard that Peter and John were teaching about Jesus, and they came upon them, having in mind that they had the motives of a sect, and placed them in custody.

Next day there came together an expanded group of rulers of high rank, scribes, and many others, as well as Annas the high priest, and Caiaphas; and they set Peter and John before them for interrogation. They asked the disciples by what means or by what name they had healed the lame man.

Peter spoke up. "I'll tell you the name that gives you grief, whether you'll acknowledge it or not. It's by the name of Jesus, the Anointed One of Nazareth, that there was strength enough to heal the lame. It's the very One whom you had crucified, whom also God has raised. Won't you have enough of ignorance and unbelief? Indeed, this verse might find you better—as you ironically refer your safety to the Scriptures—in that you have known it from a distance, but now it has found you out because it speaks of you. It says, 'The stone which the builders have rejected has become the chief cornerstone.' It will do you no good to war against His name or to apply salvation to another standard."

Peter's words did not make for enough faith or reason to persuade the high minds of the council, who, though unsettled a little by the obvious and irritating miracle (because they all knew the lame man from before), assumed only what prejudice and contentment allowed. So they consulted with each other and said, "What should we recommend? This is indeed a miracle, and the news of it has mixed with curiosity to all the people. Whatever we do, we should have this miracle retire, because who knows what lies in the rest of it. Let's therefore announce what we think of these disciples so that they may doubt their fervor when we encourage them with fear."

The council then severely threatened Peter and John, commanding them not to use or propagate the name of Jesus. Evil is voluntary enough to pass like this above, having sufficient freedom of effect in degenerated souls. This baseness or corruption, or whatever one can call it, does not think for itself; it is merely expressive of a state, unmindful of itself. The spontaneous effect of instinct does not always have a ready guide. Its crops are sporadic, and its growths come from blind intent. But sometimes the apparent random drifts of vice are led on by the passion or rage of a more sinister hand.

Satan, who had before the cross of Christ exalted himself to wage a war against the Seed of Eve and had perhaps a clarity of aim in his singular cause, had afterward, through defeat and lament, not known what he should do. When the Son of Man went by the cross and death to the underworld, He was pleased to take the keys of Hades and of Death. This was no little quest down there, because He made of Satan and his peers a great parade. Perhaps Sheol had shaken; perhaps there was a sway throughout the grey and awful scenes of dead souls; or perhaps the devils in their midst had shrieked when the Son of Man descended with His dread.

Satan had thought it hardly possible that He who died could live again. But in the passion of his rage, Satan could not see or follow the parts of God's great plan. Satan was no longer an exalted spirit, and darkness had become so affecting and had made him so demented that he was unaware that his own strike against the Son of Man would strike himself. Being so imperviously clogged, he must have had delight—if darkness can to such a thing enthuse—when he saw the Son of Man upon the cross expire. One supposes Satan had held his ethereal breath when the nails went into the cross, his triumph seeming so easy and so smooth.

It is naturally considered that he waged his war with the common device of evil, which is to reach beyond all proper laws: the trespass into violence, the advantage of theft, the supply of deceit. Perhaps he was aware of the hard conditions of breaking such natural laws. Either darkness let him only skim a notice of it, or he, in his career of revenge, was willing to degrade himself to worse penalty if he might have a chance to destroy God.

It can be accepted that a single spot on a perfect slate alters its quality inevitably. Imagine now the slate being made up entirely of perfect holiness or sinlessness; a fraction of a contaminant would alter the integrity of the whole. If God had sinned but once, the order of all things would have collapsed, and God would have toiled forever under the unkind measures of darkness.

But He who is love could not leave humanity behind in their darkness and sin, and He had come with visible intent, with a body prepared, with unfathomable zeal, to take the daring risk. Though some might not mark Him for this merit, the angels had fittingly raised their voices in a holy song to Him who had obtained success and was ascending from the dead. Indeed, it was much perfect noise, and such a clamor as one could not with a human ear imagine.

Meanwhile, Satan and his group were mute, of the kind recognized in the face of shock, since they had for a moment thought they had won against the Son of Man. The horror and the shapes of awful things had begun to meet them contrarily when they knew that God had beaten them. Partly place and partly entity, spastic Hades erupted out inhabitants. It knew not what else do to with the triumph that had walked inside of it. Or were they the train of victory of the Son of Man, who had in more than an ordinary sway brought out the captives from the dusky pits?

Afterward, Satan stirred himself together; there was no more point for victory, but what else remained but a strange, sweet, pointless wrath. Gazing out from his bleak and rocky top—some peak inside his substantial hell—he made up fancies to get back at God. Satan could not start again with sin, to make use of it for the souls of men, since God had made another way. Now, Satan thought, this dawn of Christ within the hearts of men must not enlarge into a light. Satan would rise and fight the Christ within men!

Satan had roamed Jerusalem, at first causeless, learning which was to be his best way. When he learned that this power of redemption was yielded dormant in the soft folds of preaching after the pattern of something latent and that it was conquerable by means of ignorance and unbelief, he peered about and told himself to fight. To this extent, Satan was again lord of deceit and father of lies. If he could cause mankind to shrink away from truth, he could have some command over their souls. The felicity of scorn, the dominion of force, the placidness of ignorance—all were deftly united into an offensive method.

The council tried the effects of Satan's indulgence on Peter and John; it was Satan borrowing the easy vehicle of their tirade to give off his vent. But the disciples were not displaced by this admonition, and they and the rest continued in constant prayer and preaching and in many miracles. Now Satan had the high priest as his helper, and the high priest—miserable functionary as he was—sent out guards to make an end of the apparent propaganda.

All the apostles were put in the common prison. That night, something came through the silent night, came through the chains that felt so real and permanent: an angel of the Lord defied the gloom and led them all out. The angel said, "Go back to the temple and tell the people all the words of this life."

The next morning, the high priest and all his relishing pomp took their haughty seats. Officers were sent to bring the apostles from the prison. The officers went and returned, announcing something of a wonder: that the men were not found, yet the prison was still secure and the guards were fixed at their post. The high priest, hearing this, did not erupt but acted mild, perhaps because of the strangeness of it all. While the council looked around and had no clear drift, a man came in, saying that he had the answer. The apostles were standing and preaching freely in the temple.

Resolution entered into the happy priests, who could now bear down with a double force of indulgence. Officers were sent out again to bring the men swiftly back. When the apostles were in, the council said to them, "Why are you trying us, and why are you reaching for the end of our patience? Indeed, our patience has expired; it has gone past its hour. We've told you not to preach this doctrine nor to blame His death on us."

The apostles answered, "Would we do you wrong if we do what is right? Surely we must obey God, not men."

Chapter 23

──────────── ⊰ ❈ ⊱ ────────────

The Hebrew law, which had begun with God for good, had fallen into the monopoly of the priests, scribes, and lawyers of the law, and in its falling it had been adapted to the passions of this crew. Mercy was sacrificed for judgment and chastity for penalty. Instead of a current that might lead people to hope in God, it was the viscous flow of rigid religiosity. Perhaps it was accidental, perhaps not, but legalism is unmatched in its cleverness and ample produce; it is always a concoction, and there is always something in its breath when it exhales its corrective fumes. You perceive that it wants you dead.

Meanwhile, the council was offended. They could feel their internal bones begin to twist, and their moody machinery caught sight of something that could be squashed. Now it huffed and puffed with smoke and noise, and iron made itself into molt and steam. With this effusion at their prow, the council met again and had their thoughts compared. There was only one thing they could postulate, one thing that could carry all their heat: the apostles should be dead!

A Pharisee called Gamaliel, who in temperament was more naturally warm and who was in esteem more regarded by the people, stood up and commanded the apostles to be led out of the room. He then addressed the council. "Men of Israel, consider carefully what you are about to do. Make sure justice does not become something else. Compare this situation to Theudas, who, you all remember, rose up and claimed himself to be somebody. As he drove on toward some height, his passion took hold of a number of men, swaying four hundred of them. He was slain—and his scheme too—and his followers scattered. After this came Judas of Galilee, who similarly carried some people off with his florid vision. He also died, and his group sprang away from him. Refer yourself then to these examples, because it could be that these men are not extraordinary. Let them try their hand at their venture. If it subsists in mere pretense, it won't spread into the community, but if it is from God, then you should be careful. Will patience not bring out a better thing?"

This advice made sense to the suddenly studious council, perhaps independent of their emotions, and at any rate it slowed them down to a sufficient change to let the apostles go. But sense burns bright only for a day, especially in those who are hung up in hate, and if there is any burning in such a mind, it will soon burn off the subtleties of virtue in favor of its baser state. To this extent, a persecution of the church started slowly through disputes, being rehearsed into its final felicity: the murder of a young Christian called Stephen.

The young man, Stephen, was in dispute with a group who called themselves the Synagogue of the Freedmen. These tried to beat him with ideas of doctrine, that he might fall on something he would say. In this way they went hard after him in debate, but they could not mark him on anything. The Freedmen, who were apparently freed from something, had it in them and in their motive to shackle Stephen's speech with the bondage of cultural proprieties. The deviations had to do with supposed doctrinal heresies, blasphemy, and whatever else might not fit happily into the happy norm.

At last the Freedmen grew irrepressible in conviction and hate. Their intent, now being visceral and incarnate, took hold of Stephen by the force of hand and stoned him to his death. A satisfied man had stood nearby, a Pharisee named Saul, who had observed the stoning with an approving internal nod. In fact, Saul's part in the death of Stephen was to watch the cloaks of the Freedmen stoners who needed their alacrity.

Zeal does not look back into the past, nor even to the present moment, when it treads and stomps a little in its advancing pace. No, zeal's crown lies ahead; there is no such thing as rest. Combined with zeal and religiosity, Saul went on to argue against the church—or really against anything that rose above his moral canon. That same day, a great persecution began against the Christians. It seemed as if Saul had the entire command over the offensive. He created havoc in Jerusalem, shutting his eyes to the howls and screams and blood of the Christians he dragged from house after house and tossed into the prison.

His apparent success in Jerusalem mingled with greater aspirations; he wanted to try the effect of violence on the Christians in Damascus. As part of this expectation, he obtained letters of approval from the high priest, which might give his inquisition the necessary support and reign. Having obtained this, he set out with a group of men on the road to Damascus. On the way, he daydreamed brightly of accomplishment, but suddenly, within the glimmers of his private little light, another light fell on him from the sky. Saul knew not in what terms to acknowledge this strange and supernatural force, and being bewildered and without clear sense, he fell to the ground.

Out of the light, a voice spoke, saying, "Saul, why are you persecuting Me?"

Now the religious plough that had shaped Saul's mind throughout his years had left its furrows and its heaps, and a speaking God was long lost and somewhere underground. The dry propensity of his mind's soil could not deny the shock of sudden rain, and in fright it gave a portion up to it. There was nowhere to go, and his mechanized mind, unable to find its malignant sources in the presence of this God, creaked out, as if without oil, a successful and an anguished sputter: "Who are you, Lord?"

The Lord answered, "I am Jesus, whom you are persecuting. It must be hard for you to kick against the goads."

It is amazing how the once rigid Saul changed, how suddenly he could go over himself, how quickly he could adjust the course that streamed in him. In an instant, he slew himself, as it were, and in that instant he was left a sterile remnant, which he offered up to this intense God. And Saul asked, trembling, "Lord, what do you want me to do?"

Jesus said, "Go into the city, and I'll tell you what to do there."

The blazing light—and understanding also—had passed by the group of men who were with Saul on the road, as they were confounded by hearing only a muffled voice in the air. The peculiar effects of the intruding light caused a sort of blindness to the eyes of Saul, and the men did not know how to admit this occurrence into the common sense of things. Yet they were rendered sympathetic to these strange eyelids of Saul, which had now grown into a crusty type of covering scale. It was thought better to move away from this striking sky and on to Damascus, where they would grieve out the blindness or wait for something new.

About this time—well, really, it was three days later—a man named Ananias sat in meditative ease, perhaps in prayer, because he was a follower of Christ. In his mind, some other beam, a vision, had begun to shine pale through the curtain of his flesh. The burden of this veil caused him to see formless at first, but then—as though with faith that forced the old love of his flesh to look away—he saw and heard a gentle voice of God. The Lord said to Ananias, "Go to a street called Straight to the house of someone called Judas and inquire after Saul of Tarsus, because in a vision he has seen you come."

Ananias answered in mild contest, "Lord, I've heard about this man, how he has been throwing us about, his angry way, his angry letters from the priests."

The Lord said, "Go anyway. The goal is not your death, because he's allied now with Us."

Ananias went there and placed his hands on Saul and healed him, and the scales on his eyes were compelled to drop. So Saul got up and passed by all his past, because he immediately went into the synagogues, preaching this Jesus as the Christ.

After a few days, the intransigent Jews of the city had had enough of this new product of Saul. As it is true for many, murder needs no special womb, and these men needed little to birth the demand for blood. After rehearsing the idea into a ripened pitch, they set out to the gates of the city, watching day and night that they might substitute their rage into a blow. Such intense and heated air could not hold its fever from the wind, and soon the rumor of the plot was told to Saul. Courage does not deride wisdom, nor the prudence of escape, and Saul was let down the wall through the guise of an innocent basket.

Truth took its first place in the mind of Saul, and he was not deterred by the animosity that lurked at every expedient corner. He returned conspicuously to Jerusalem. Fear was not forgotten easily, and the Christians in Jerusalem were haunted with the notion that this Saul, who had just arrived in Jerusalem, would use his new confession as a crafty front. Where they assigned their impulses to draw back from him, another disciple named Barnabas took matters into his reconciling hands, taking Saul to the apostles to candidly hear his claim and to do away with the exaggeration of anxiety. As for the apostles, they left their doubts, giving full credit to Saul's encounter with the Lord. Having been accepted by them, Saul began, as though with a continuous force of energy, to preach the Way in Jerusalem.

At one such event, he presumed to dispute against Hellenists, who took it as a slight. Besides this, the Hellenists took a clear perception for the cause of murder. The defect of their cause and thought was strangely absent. At any rate, they were ready to spew out their infernal hate in the name of their doctrinal good, and they sought Saul out for a deadly use. But Saul found out, and the deadly dart of the Hellenists remained a thought, the bow never being bent.

With danger behind them and readiness within, the indomitable Christians scattered and preached as far away as Phoenicia, Cyprus, and Antioch. Meanwhile, the corrupted Herod saw some meaning in this human chase and supposed to harass the Christians a little bit. That demanded blood and a discriminate scene. To this end, the distinguished John, brother of James, was caught and killed. John's death caused excitement and an approving commentary from the Jews. The susceptible Herod could not handle the consuming flattery that praised his bloody hand, and he sprang enthusiastically forth, grabbing Peter next for an arrest.

All are born with conscience, this to the aching annoyance of the relishing wicked who quickly wrench themselves free from this corrective minister by way of a self-applied, searing iron. With this critic locked up, crusted up, the depraved and foolish mind can better consort with whatever gives it bliss. As for Herod, he knew not the reason he was for himself, nor why he hungered for the outward praise that had stitched traceries right into his needing heart. Morning came, and Herod's thoughts were lost in the happiness of Peter's imminent execution.

Later in the day, Herod's thoughts passed from happiness to anger. It is never good for power to surpass a man, and indeed how terrible for a mind to suppose so much power or for power to suppose itself in man. And though one may yearn for it as a safety, power will not crown one to an equal state.

It came about that Herod, sitting proud and feeling comprehensive, was told that Peter was gone. Indeed, the squads of guards spared not to search. Now Peter was not found, because an angel had taken him outside by night. Fury grew inside Herod's breast, something brutish, something of a beast. As there was no space for any good, he ordered all the guards to death; and as he had no longer any common way to cope, he left that sulking place in something of a tizzy and moved to Caesarea to wait the sulking out.

Some time after, and for whatever reason, Herod had another fit of passion—the pilfered privilege of power—and was angry at someone else: in this case, the people of Tyre and Sidon. These people knew this species of authority and anger that was on their account, and they knew that it could only be placated by the less-than-novel move of flattery. What gave them additional incentive to make use of this dubious minister was that their country depended on a food supply from Herod's treasuries. They dared to befriend Blastus, the king's personal aid, in order to have their plea for peace ascend to the ear of Herod. Now Herod did not give in entirely, only giving some proportion of his anger to the interest of bemusement and leaving some over for a planned reprimand, which, if all went well, would shame the people sufficiently into groveling deference.

The day was set for the grand oration, with Herod lifted up on his throne in shining royal apparel and the people of Tyre and Sidon aggregating, tear-faced in dust. Herod began speaking, sounding rough and justified, and sounding like he wanted them to be aware. His words clashed with intermingling possibilities of clemency, and his eyes dropped down now and then to them who thawed beneath his baking beam.

In spite of their offended state, the quivering people knew how to overthrow the quarrel, and they began to shout at every pause in Herod's roar: "It's the voice of a god, not a man!"

It is never wise to submit or be tempted by this sort of ridiculous congratulations. At any rate, Herod seemed to have had a general taste for it and was struck immediately by a scornful angel. The plague was proportionate to Herod's sin, and in him were found worms that ate him, and he died.

Meanwhile, Saul, who was also called Paul, found himself in Antioch. While he was praying and fasting with a group of Christians, the Holy Spirit spoke to them to separate Barnabas and Paul for the work of the ministry. And being sent out by the Holy Spirit, Paul and Barnabas traveled subsequently to Seleucia, taking a boat from there to Cyprus, and at length arrived at Salamis, where they started preaching the word of God.

In time they ended up in Paphos, where they encountered the censure of a sorcerer whose name was Bar-Jesus. This sorcerer had broken into the confidence of Sergius Paulus, a proconsul of Paphos, and worked himself into a whispering sidekick. When the proconsul took an interest in Paul and Barnabas and called to hear what they were saying, this Bar-Jesus wished to fix the conversation into gall. Whatever Paul would say, the sorcerer would oppose, subtracting it to false doctrines and words that time would soon burn out as ash and wind. But meekness is not without defense or strength, and Paul, full of the Holy Spirit, said to the sorcerer, "How can I call you by your name? Because right across your mind lies every deceit, every strength that handles fraud. Will you never stop driving on with this perversion of the Lord? Therefore judgment will this time reach beyond its mercy and judge you blind for a certain length of time!"

Bar-Jesus was struck immediately with something of a mist over his eyes, and he had nowhere to go and no resource for himself except the hand of some aid who led him from the room.

When at last the proconsul was insulated from the molestations of the sorcerer, he believed, being astonished at the miracle and the teachings of the Way.

In time, Paul and Barnabas traveled on—sometimes as ministers, sometimes as fugitives—but always they went on, always at the plough. A variety of soil were found: some fallow, some delicate, some timid, and some relaxed by hospitality. There were some who entertained the seeds sown for amusement and some who had more peculiar reflexes, as in the case of the people of Lystra.

There was a man in Lystra, crippled from birth, who sat listening to Paul and Barnabas. His impatient hope had faith, and when Paul saw this in his eyes, he said to the man, "Stand up on your feet!"

His legs, which had lain so long in impotence, leaped up straight, and he began to walk in ecstasy. The people of Lystra saw the unbearable miracle, and being astonished, said to each other, "The gods have come down to us in the forms of men!"

They exclaimed this in conjunction with their religion and handed Barnabas the name of Zeus and Paul the name of Hermes. The priest of Zeus, in his crowded thoughts and frenzy, rushed livestock and garlands to the gates that he might contrive to please his god through the mortal service of a sacrifice. When Paul and Barnabas heard of this improper zeal, they ran into the crowd and asked them to stop, saying, "We are men just like you. Rather, turn from these useless things and worship the living God."

Perhaps the people did not hear, or they took it for a modesty, because Paul and Barnabas could hardly stop their eager thrusts. At that exact time, Jews from Antioch and Iconium arrived at Lystra, and they had better luck to calm the running feet of the zealots. Words of a ruse were heard above the words of truth, and the moody crowd shortened the surprise of an incarnated Zeus or Hermes into the size of a stone, since they took these objects for their new emotion and stoned Paul to what they thought was death.

Paul's apparent death calmed the people's irritation, and they had just enough quarrel left in them to drag Paul's body outside of the city to let nature have the last stroke and be done with him forever. Their intent did not breach his life, and he got up and went back into the city. The next day, he and Barnabas left.

Once, in Athens, Paul was dismayed at the city's culture, which, by the curiosity of unraveling life or truth, was given over to ubiquitous idolatry. From this rose many statues, temples, and various sacred objects, each to their invisible spirits and preferring gods. Paul started reasoning daily with the worshippers who happened to be around. Certain Epicurean and Stoic philosophers took note of Paul's exchange and invited him to speak at the Areopagus. Now some were saying, "What is he going on for, ranting like that?" And others said, "He seems to talk about some foreign god."

All the Athenians and foreigners who were there had a rather pointed vanity of mind, a curiosity of a kind that always looked for something new to talk about; such was the spirit of their culture at the time. Then Paul stood in the Areopagus and said, "People of Athens, it appears to me that you are all religious. Even your city itself is marked by this quality. I see objects of worship enlarged all over for this use. It happened that I came across an altar with this inscription: To the Unknown God. If you're willing, I'd like to give you some news of Him.

"He's not bound by the earth or even stars, nor does He answer from a temple or an object made by human hands. These can't guide Him or invoke Him as one might appease and conjure up a spirit from its haunt. Nor is He in need of some extra strength, some help from man to make Him stand a little higher. Indeed, He is Lord of earth and heaven, has made all things, has made man, has given life and breath to all. We all have our growth from Him, by one blood by which He made all mankind. It's His way to place us where we are, that we may grope for Him and find Him and be no longer lost. He is not hard to find, not like a spirit from the underworld. No, He comes forward when His name is called.

"But then He is spirit still and commits Himself to spirit. Indeed, He drifts not around like a weak wind seeking for a hollow, nor does He sleep in daytime that He might at night and ghostlike make surprises. He isn't far from us; we move in Him and have our being. It's as some of your own poets even have said, 'He has birthed us into children.' Since we are His offspring, and since we are aware of our own liveliness, how can we then appropriate the divine nature into the recesses of things made by human hands—gold or silver or stone shaped to stuff a spirit in? God has overlooked this vanity, but now He calls on all to be done with all this dreaminess, to take away the stony idol and its ungrown god and start afresh with God. He has appointed a day when He will no longer wait and talk this out but will hold all people accountable to righteousness and judge them by a Man whom He has ordained and raised from the dead."

The idea of resurrection was to the minds of the audience what water is to fire, and toward Paul and his message they were no longer that keen.

Being deterred by their unbelief, Paul left, and in time he arrived at Ephesus. Finding some followers of Christ there, he asked them as to the matter of the Holy Spirit, whether they had received the Holy Spirit when they came to believe. They confessed themselves to be confused by the question, saying that they knew about Christ but that this Holy Spirit was outside of their common view.

Now this was an open-minded group and hungry, as it were; they could handle a new idea. They were aware of their old lives, of their withered walk round and round the selfsame track. These disciples at Ephesus had had a taste of truth. They had sat enough at the station of their life and had had enough of the locomotion of their humdrum train. On the grounds of openness and faith, they believed Paul and received the Holy Spirit, speaking in tongues and prophesying.

To the people of Ephesus, Paul devoted much time and conveyed himself for about two years at the school of Tyrannus. In this way, the message of the new life spread throughout Asia. The believers were not just dependent on the words of Paul, but their faith could stand at the same time on the extraordinary miracles that God worked through him—even to the point where the power within Paul was transferred to handkerchiefs and other anointed objects that functioned then as something of a bridge or conveyer that, when placed on people, passed on to them healings and deliverances.

Some Jewish exorcists, who were perhaps tired of the impotence of their own rituals, were desirous of a taste of the peculiar power they saw by the hands of Paul. Though their hearts could not answer to any acceptance of the message of the Christ, their minds could not deny the power of it for the sake of the evidence. To this extent, they exorcised demons by means of a peculiar move, saying to the demons, "We exorcise you by this Jesus whom Paul preaches!"

In one such instance, the seven sons of Sceva, a Jewish chief priest, called out loud to a demon in this way. But the evil spirit answered them, saying, "I know this Jesus, and I know this Paul, but who are you?"

Then the man who was possessed grabbed these sons with incomparable rage and strength, overpowering them and throwing them around. When the sons saw that they could not prevail in authority or combat, and when they were torn, naked and wounded, they fled in desperation.

Chapter 24

Paul had it in mind to give attention to Jerusalem, and after a few years he returned there. The report of Paul to the elders of the church in Jerusalem was received with interest and with taste, and they glorified God for the spread of the Word. James and the other elders cautioned Paul that many of the Jewish Christians—for there had been by this time many converted—still pronounced Paul's name with the cold and chill reserved for heretics. Indeed, the Jewish Christians had no other grounds for their accusations. They were convinced that Paul was the pilot of their valid anger, that he had gone on his own and partial way, offending the Jews and the Mosaic law in his worldwide parade, teaching even that circumcision was no longer necessary.

The solution, the elders discreetly advised, was to give the Jewish Christians no cause for any such impression, but indeed and instead to promote that Paul was an upright man, walking in the constraint and respect of the Law. In order to bring the perception of the Jewish Christians into this proximity, a nifty solution was already nearby: four men had already taken a religious vow and would shave their heads and do a purification. Therefore, if Paul could join them in the ritual, it might set the circumstance in better order.

James also informed Paul that the Gentile Christians were considered in some way insulated from the reach of the Law, and that no more than a few rules were applied to them. They concluded that the Gentiles needed only to keep themselves from idols, blood, strangled flesh, and sexual depravities.

Having anger for a neighbor is not good for any person, and Paul, one supposes, thought it enough to compromise for the sake of peace and for the Jewish Christians' consciences' sake, inasmuch as he agreed to the ritual. Now, when the thing was going through and Paul was in the temple performing the ritual, some Jews spotted him and leered at him with squinted eyes. These men thought it better to serve proprieties than love, and they began to stir up the people of the city to take part in their perceived righteous fit. When their anger grew out of proportion to their shouts and the figures of their fists, they grabbed Paul with the intent to kill him.

News of an uproar came to the commander of the garrison of Jerusalem, that the whole city was in a will of its own. The commander hastily grabbed some soldiers and ran toward the largest and most obvious cluster of mobs, as it seemed reasonable for chaos to arrange its source about there. A pleasure-house of violence compelled fair hands into something more like claws. A plea from Paul went up toward what was left of humanness, but the mob's actions and a spirit of rage and hate functioned first to intercept his plea and to deny a motive that might bring about a calm. When the commander and his soldiers arrived, the upstaged crowd stopped beating Paul, shrinking away and deferring, animal-like, to the force and fear of the soldiers. Guilt was assumed by the appearance of it all, and Paul was put in chains right there and then. The commander then enquired as to the reason for the crowd's complaint, but it appeared to him that none of them could say what they had meant with their fists and there seemed no exact purpose for beating him. One was saying this and another that; in short, the circumstance was divided. At length, when the commander could not get ahead with his inquiry, he sent Paul bound to the barracks.

When the mind cannot rely on older thoughts, some youthful thought breaks in to stretch itself as long. In this instance, the commander had no warders to guard his patience and reserve, and suspicion entered in and took the place of doubt. So the commander said to Paul, "Are you the Egyptian fellow who accosted the empire some time ago by making trouble through a rebellion and leading four thousand assassins into the wilderness?"

Paul answered him, "No, I am a Jew from Tarsus in Cicilia."

The commander nonetheless thought there was something more to it all, thinking the uproar of the people and their shouts did not rise for nothing. Suspicion in those days was reasoned away through the use of an easy intervention, the exercise of torture; therefore the commander ordered Paul to be scourged. Although this might have been a solace for the perplexed commander, it was not for Paul, who thought it not worth it to take a fruitless beating. Paul said to the centurion who was preparing his pain, "Is it lawful to punish a Roman who has not yet been found guilty?"

On hearing this, the centurion was no longer in full confidence of his task, and he went to the commander and said to him, "You should be careful what you do to this man, because he is a Roman."

The commander then returned to Paul to find it out by his own words.

"Are you a Roman?" he asked.

Paul answered that he was. The commander said, "I had to give up a great sum to buy my citizenship."

Paul answered, "But I was born so."

When those around Paul, the interrogators, heard this, they stood immediately back, fearing the consequence of what they almost had done. Since the truth, from the commander's point of view, could not be trod out with the pressings of pain, he was obliged to unbind Paul and refer him to the opinion of the Sanhedrin the next day.

The Sanhedrin sat unnaturally as priests, being naturally aloof, but the setup was convenient to the interrogation of Paul, who was brought before them the next day. The Sanhedrin stared at him, and he at them. Paul began, "My brothers, we each have in our obedience to truth the keeping of conscience, and I'm telling you that all my life I've lived without a bad conscience before God."

This statement was one thing too much for one of the listening priests, who thought the words sloped too close to sin, came too close to the grounds of his private law, and he ordered a guard to hit Paul on his mouth. Paul said to the priest, "Do you have the Law all to yourself that you can break it? Will God not strike you for what you just did? You're a whitewashed wall, being so full of the line-upon-line and dense from the heaps of words that you let no one pass toward the truth!"

Some who were standing by said to Paul, "Do you know to whom who are speaking? It's the high priest you are maligning."

Paul answered, "It's something I didn't know, my brothers; and if I had to answer to him again, I would have said it differently, since it is in the Law that one shouldn't speak evil of the ruler of the people of God."

Perhaps Paul perceived the direction of the interrogation was playing out as a drama and that he needed not play along for the benefit of the stage. The council existed in a constrained coalition of Pharisees and Sadducees. Both groups staunchly gave themselves and their convictions to the Law, yet there was some disparity as to matters of cardinal doctrine, which no doubt, from time to time, caused friction against each other.

The Sadducees had in the error of their way chained down the supernatural as mere windy thoughts of ghosts, and the entities of angels to the emptiness of fallacy, because they did not believe in such. The same view was held out to the resurrection of man, which they opposed and dissolved into a bleak and ossified view of mankind's hopes. And Paul, being aware of this distinction, said, "I'm a Pharisee; I'm being judged for my belief in the resurrection."

The common air against Paul had its end right there, and a dissention rose with a growing angry mood. The Pharisees would say, "Should we be so swift to say our mind against him? What if a spirit or an angel thought it good to speak to him?"

The Sadducees could not move on that and argued more. The quarrel turned quite rough, and each faction started to reach for Paul, as if to make their reason clear by grabbing him and shoving him to their side. The commander, who was watching, knew this was the making of a bad argument, and fearing Paul would soon be injured by the callow tussle, he sent soldiers in to take Paul back to the barracks.

Who knows where Paul was in his heart? From deep below, perhaps resilience might have risen up, or perhaps a mad, discouraged thought floated on the surface of ideas. God, though only light, is not always as a midday sun; it is His glory to have His shine in shadows cloaked. At midnight, then, His whisper spoke. "Be well, Paul, and of a better mood, because as you have testified of Me here, you will also testify of Me in Rome."

The next day, there were some Jews who got together. Their passions had gone up to their minds and won, and it followed that they bound themselves by an uncompromising oath, and to make the oath better, they swore not to eat any food until they had killed Paul. This required a scheme and a conspiracy. The oscillating elders and chief priests would do well for the mutual scheme, and it was agreed that elders and priests would request to recall Paul back the next day for questioning, by reason of coming to the bottom of it all, in the pretense of sincerity and good intention. The hungry plotters assured the elders and priests that the plan would be divided halfway, that halfway on his way, Paul will be taken down.

How would they keep their secret low, when their hopes were so inversely high? Some excitement in their inflated breasts exhaled the dark thought to the air, and Paul's sister's son caught the rank breath of it. On hearing this, he went to Paul and told him of the plot. Paul was not going to take the news with a groan, and he called one of the centurions, saying, "A young man has something to say to the commander."

When the young man was brought in, the commander took him aside and asked, "What do you want to tell me?"

The young man said, "There's something that I've overheard, of forty men who have conspired by an oath to kill Paul, and these have taken the priests in on their scheme. They'll request Paul for questioning, but the difference is that they lie in wait for him and mean for his death instead."

The commander told the young man, "Don't tell anyone what you've told me."

The commander admitted the hearsay as truth, and he coolly and immediately conceived a way out. If the Jews' plot were swift, his would be swifter; if they came audacious, he would meet their dare with hellish force. He then called two centurions and asked them to prepare two hundred soldiers, seventy horsemen, and two hundred spearmen, and to provide a mount for Paul—and to set out at three in the morning for Caesarea, for Felix the governor. A letter would accompany the troops by the commander, written as follows:

Claudius Lysias,

To the most excellent governor Felix: Greetings.

The Jews somehow took this man by force and were ready to kill him. However, I came upon him and rescued him with the help of my troops, having learned that he was a Roman. I had brought him then to their council to see what the attention was all about, but their accusations were partial to matters of their own law, and I did not notice anything that gave reason for death or even chains. When I was informed that the

Jews had conspired to kill him by whatever means, I sent him immediately to your care. I have also told his accusers to bring the charges to you.

Farewell.

Paul was hustled to Felix in this way, and the murder was averted. Five days later, Ananias the high priest and his group came down to Felix the governor. They had brought with them one Tertullus, a man who was an orator of sorts, who apparently did not get wind-broken in long speech and could take up any argument into his turn. When Tertullus was called to speak in front of the hearing on Paul, he said, "I'd like to say how suitable it is for us to be before you, most noble Felix, because of the felicity of your governing, seeing that your foresight has found for us much peace and prosperity. Thank you for this. I really don't wish to bother your high state and busy situation with any drudgery, so I'll come right to the point and use what few words your courtesy allows.

"We found this man, Paul, a self-proceeding plague; he has spread himself throughout the world, being loud in his dissenting voice. You must understand then that we cannot help but feel his effect without unease. For whatever reason, he and his sect of Nazarenes—he is the ringleader—want to make themselves relevant to us through much antagonism. He even entered and used with contempt the temple to drive his epidemic on. But we couldn't let him and finally caught him. Now we were ready to attend to him and judge him according to our law, but the commander Lysias came violently upon us and seized him from us. You can examine this man and see for yourself that our accusations are true."

Afterward, it was Paul's turn, and Felix unpaused him by a nod of his head. Paul said, "I know you've not been a recent judge. Therefore, I don't mind to hope in you when I answer these accusations. It was about twelve days ago that I went to Jerusalem.

I gave them no occasion to raise themselves against me. I knew that I was always watched, as I could see it in their eyes. You need not ask about the Way; it is true that I am joined with them and believe, therefore, in the God of my fathers and in the law and the prophets. What is to my accusers a protesting wedge, is to the Way the fulfillment of our identical hope, the resurrection of the dead. I was indeed in the temple when they grabbed me. I wasn't stirring up things as they accuse me of but was passive, busy with a ritual of purification. Let my accusers say exactly what impressed them so badly about me, except maybe of what I said when they seized me—that I believe in the resurrection of the dead."

The verdict of a patient judge lies far off, and Felix postponed the hearing, wishing, one supposes, to come to the end of it by slow degrees. There must have been a sense of fairness from it all, because though Paul was kept in jail, he was given liberties, and his friends could be received.

After a few days, Felix had curiosity as his theme—perhaps on account of his wife, Drusilla, who was Jewish—and feeling voluble, he sent for Paul again.

As Paul talked about faith in Christ—his discourse being in common with ideas of righteousness and judgment—Felix became afraid of what he heard, and he sent Paul away for another time. Felix's mode was for ignorance. What if new faith woke him reluctantly? At any rate, it was a curious subject for him, and he sent for Paul often and for short intervals, testing the waters from safe ground. At the same time, cunning fellow that Felix was, he hoped that Paul might for a moment forget all this righteous stuff and bring a bribe for his release. But strange Paul never gave him what he wished for, and he, without pity, kept Paul for two years in this state.

Small crowns grow not always bigger. More often, in fact, these unsteady honors answer to the tide of change. Something burns alongside short life and gives random graves to some and long and storied lives to others. Sick mankind sees sickness yet hopes on the force of fate. Indeed the grass—as the rich and wise

Solomon said—withers away to make way for the new. What did the old thing do to be so wrong and weak? Here comes a new, usurping thing. And so there is in life some swift and restless wind that swoops down on scattered man. It does not care if it is despised when it contends with order and with peace.

This capricious wind passed into the life of Felix about two years later, and Porcius Festus succeeded him. Felix had left Paul in jail as part of his last duties, answering a favor to the Jews. Now hate cannot be buried in a grave, as the heart does not allow for its abortion; and the chief priests and leaders of the Jews were after two years still aggravated to the point of murder. When Porcius Festus came into power, they contended again against Paul, asking Festus for a favor: to send Paul back to Jerusalem. The pretense and sentiment were was the same. They would lie in wait for Paul and kill him on his way. But Festus said no, wanting to try his own judicial temper on the infamous case.

Another hearing was called, and both Paul and the Jews were present, with potent Festus on the judgment seat. Darkness had had two years to spawn its imps and fiendish sprites, and these poured out hellishly in the form of words, made-up accusations against Paul. Accusation is what the Devil does best; it is the potent edge of his limp sword. All of mankind sinks under this sin, yet they blast each other with its trouble. At length Festus asked Paul if he was willing to go to Jerusalem to be judged there before Festus. But Paul turned it down with curt impatience, making an appeal to be heard before Caesar himself.

Upon this motive, then, Paul began his journey to Italy. It was not meant to be a wonderful voyage; the stern eyes of the Roman guards would be for Paul a continuous reminder of his bonds. With Paul were other prisoners as well, all under the power and fostering care of one named Julius, a centurion of the Augustan Regiment. This Julius appeared not to be only a minister of the sword; he had enough heart to condescend to decency toward Paul and allowed him to be cared for by his co-traveling friends.

They at length put out to sea by ship and next day arrived at Sidon. Then they sailed past Cyprus to Myra, a city of Lycia. Their ship could not boast, for whatever reason, to carry them all the way to Italy, and the centurion found an Alexandrian ship that could contend with the seas for the last part of their voyage. They boarded the new ship and sailed with strain onward, the wind being in a thwarting temper, and arrived exhausted at a port beautifully named Fair Havens.

Though the little port aspired by its name to bring rest, it was not enough, nor was it suitable to winter in. As the centurion was eyeing the sea again, Paul warned him of it, saying he perceived there was no way to win against the season, that there would be loss of ship and crew. The centurion regarded the advice of the helmsman and the owner of the ship instead, who told him there was yet time to be brave and reach Phoenix, a harbor of Crete, before winter.

The sea wind kept her older tempests sleeping sound and sent its younger offspring first to sniff about with gentle searching sweeps. And when the centurion saw the kind wind, his anxieties were dispersed by the oppression of his excitement. So they all set sail again, staying close to Crete along the way, just in case.

That which began brave ran into fear, because the sea wind found out this audacious little ship and was in mood for war. Soon a tempestuous wind came down on them. The crew did not wish to be dead; they grabbed things and muscled about against the untamed wind. They realized they could not with their arms make way, and they gave up and let the ship drive on its own and with the wind. When the wind felt the ship in its grisly grasp, it steered it to a bank, the Syrtis Sands, to spit it out, to toss and wreck it on the bank. The suspecting sailors saw what might be coming, and they struck the sails again that they might use the aggravation of the wind to overcome the bank. The limbless wind could not help this consequence and only took the ship deeper into the sea. The resilient crew felt this was not their lot, and they fought on, lightening the load of the ship. On the third day, the wind and lapping waves refused to dwindle. With moans, the boat complained, and the crew were forced to throw the tackle overboard.

It was indeed strange weather intended for them, and the crew was puzzled as to why the wind carried on so unequally; for days and days it went on exceptionally, even blotting out the sky and the stars. Time takes patience and misery hope, and the crew were converted to despair, to the picture of their private, drowning deaths. Paul stood up and said, "Don't have this death as your admitted future. Last night an angel of the God whom I serve appeared to me, saying that I'll indeed be brought before Caesar and that God has insured all your lives on my account. Let this news bring with it hope, because I'm certain it will be as it was told to me—only the ship will be lost."

For fourteen days the sea heaved up and down, each wave a gaping mouth that surged and snapped at the bows of the skipping ship; yet the waters did not have hunger or strength enough to take it sunken to its deep. In this way the ship went up and down the Adriatic sea. Then around midnight the sailors perceived that they were drifting toward some land. Their suspicion was confirmed by the soundings, which were twenty fathoms at first, and then fifteen. The judgment and experience were that the nearby land, like many shores, had rehearsed itself with outer rocks like outer roots before it sloped more even into sand. Anchors were dropped to steady the ship, and all the crew sat waiting and gazing out for the break of day.

For whatever reason, the sailors had misgivings about the patient plan and agreed amongst themselves to escape on a skiff. Now the sailors had let down the skiff as though they were letting down the anchors, but the alert Paul noticed their mischievous project and told the centurion and the soldiers. The soldiers moved quickly and cut the ropes of the skiff, while the distraught sailors huddled implicitly back into the ship.

There were two hundred and seventy-six people on board in total, and when morning came they all ate and threw the rest of the wheat into the sea. To survive the sea, it was thought best to loose the rudder ropes, hoist the mainsail, and run the ship into the bay. Their last-ditch effort was not exempt from the mood of the murderous sea, and a vexing rock caught them on the way. The exultant rock pierced into the prow, and the waves lapped onto the stern, and soon the ship, made up of so much strength and patient will, gave up its wood and shape and moaned its way to death.

The soldiers had in this strange moment still will enough to defend their role as guards, and fearing the prisoners might swim away, they set out to kill them. The centurion, who had in his mind a place for Paul, prevented them, ordering all who wished to live to dive into the sea and beat their sole strength against the waves, and those who were unable to swim to dare on out with boards and planks or whatever they could find.

When dead men drown, their ghosts rise up within the spraying foam, but on this day there were no naked, floating shapes that seaward drifted. No, the angel who took care of them laughed off the toothless edge of sea. In this way they were all rescued and collected on the beach.

The local people of Malta—the island's name—had watched their accident and their splattering to the land and, perceiving their ordeal, were very kind to them and took care of them. What was left out of comfort was the impingement of the cold, and some left over pelting by the rain.

A fire was started on the beach, and diligent Paul gathered the sticks. As Paul placed a bundle on the flames, a snake came out because of the heat. The snake did not take escape for a concession and instead fiercely latched itself onto Paul's hand. The snake found no life by that, because Paul shook it off into the fire. Now the local people watched this askance and thought that Paul was no doubt a murderer, that justice was unwilling to resign against him, that it had sent the snake to finish off what the sea had meant to do. The locals kept looking at him to see when he would swell and drop, but their apprehension never fitted their forecast; Paul was fine. This led the natives to an inward spell of abstraction, a private effusion of marvel, and an inevitable belief that Paul was a sort of demigod.

Prominent on the island, a man named Publius took note of the destitute survivors and invited and entertained them for a few days. Publius' father was ill from a type of dysentery and Paul healed him.

Hope is not as blind as faith for flesh, and the natives of the island, on hearing of this, brought their sick to Paul, who healed them all. They spent three months in this way on the island.

Spring came in when winter left, and out of spring, dim things stirred back to shine. It told of future's musts, of plans that must have deeds, and of an Alexandrian ship that would take them safely to Rome.

When Paul and the others arrived at last at Rome, he was delivered to the captain of the guard with the other prisoners. Paul was in this dark post blessed, because he was allowed to live by himself. Only a soldier was given to him to enforce at least a proportion of captivity. Paul did not take his remote corner in Rome and in life as an excuse, and the captive recess that his opposition had placed him in was turned by God into an emphatic advantage. With bold determination, Paul engaged everyone and anyone around him, preaching the gospel in Rome and writing letters that would forever endure, upsetting and altering forever the course of history and kingdoms that might otherwise have lain prone in their orthodoxy and the hollowness of Satan's artifice.

It should be understood that not all Paul's letters were written on the dismal table of his chains in Rome. There were some written years earlier and some afterward, when his counsel had condensed in ink onto the scrolls sent out to the church and to the entire world.

Chapter 25

— ❧ ✖ ❧ —

A letter of Paul to the Romans:

To the people of Rome, to you who are indeed loved by God, to you who are called to be saints: grace and peace from God our Father and the Lord Jesus Christ.

I am a bondservant of Jesus Christ to this message of peace, a peace which you may find strange, having been so long used to the familiarity of guilt. But He has all along promised this message through the old prophets and Scriptures concerning Jesus the Messiah, whom He has declared to be the Son of God.

I am not ashamed of this message of Christ. It is the power of God to save everyone who believes it. Make every effort to include yourself in this salvation. This salvation is for everyone. It speaks of a righteousness, a new sinless state that is by faith. Now you all have in some deep and bottled vessel of your soul a sense of the wrath of God. Indeed, it is true that this holy God with troubled heart cannot help but break out against the ungodliness of men and their unrighteousness, whereby and in delight thereof, they had set God's light as a distant night and their indulgent moon as their sun. But this suppression reaches not to the level of an excuse, and it will not let them off the hook.

In the creation of the world, the reference to God—if one would only earnestly go there for a receptive look—is apparent. Through the years, mankind inertly preferred the pleasing caricatures of the eternal impulse, the dark and whispering muses, over the voice of God, and they soon learned the business of idolatry. Therefore, God reluctantly gave them over to their promoted resignation, by which they all became degraded to a futility of mind, to the chains of dark thoughts, to the circumference of created things instead of the Creator.

The Jews have taken their notion and their redemption to the Law of Moses. They have gone on with effort—without thinking reflectively that the Law has assumed itself higher than their struggle against sin, that the Law has far more ambition than their hope and labor have. As for the other peoples who might suspect themselves free from the hammer of the Law, another law appears to their surprise: an innate and common law of right and wrong, something written on the heart that rises up and accuses them. But either way, and with either law, mankind is full of awful works. You, teachers of the Law, you think yourself stronger than the thing you teach, but the Law and the conscience know better. They have felt your proud pulse and have known the delusion that you follow; they have remembered the thousand sins you have sinned; they have known that your labors are not enough of a hiding place in the day when God comes to judge the secrets of your hearts.

Take for instance circumcision, which is the peculiar rite under the Law of Moses and is profitable only if you are capable of keeping the Law in its entirety. Therefore, God, who remembered that you are unable, has aimed for something better and higher—a circumcision of the heart, as it were, something above flesh, something spirit. Now there is the hard stance of the proud who do not wish to wet their feet with the dew on the new grass. No, the proximity of the Day frustrates them, and they wish for the dryness of old times. They are familiar with the dusty and the sapless, and they quickly discard the moistness of the new day as something strange and oceanic.

Sin does live in both Jew and Greek, and none can reason away their unrighteous state; all have turned away. Even if you hold up somewhat of a succession of good efforts in obedience to the Law or the satisfaction of your watchful conscience, what will be the outcome? It cannot translate you into true righteousness. It is better that you come to a collision of your old mindset, that you give up the resilient patience of your hard works, that you recognize that you really have not known the way of peace. But a new life spring has appeared to all mankind, a water that takes into account the Law and all sin, a medicine that does not need your help. This righteousness, even the righteousness of God, is deemed yours simply through your belief in Jesus Christ.

One looks for things to boast about, for one's own might to be mentioned in praising terms in heaven or by God, but it is now a fasting time for any boast, a grim time for muscling, self-supposing work. If you feel your scheme of salvation must revolve around a law, then settle yourself and your working arm, and take up the law of faith like Abraham, who believed God and was accounted as righteous. Working for worth is so affecting to mankind. What is better for the pleasure of pride? But the plan for mankind's redemption plays out without their strength. Indeed, because mankind cannot live by their own strength, Christ came to live and make the merit.

Some good person on edge might scarcely die for someone else, and if at all, it will likely be for someone good. Yet we see God's great love for man when He with grief and joy sent Christ to die for us while we were still sinners. This is a simple thing to understand; I will not overbuild the concept with aggregating philosophy. If we were reconciled to God while yet stained and estranged, it is to be imagined how much more we will receive of His life and glory when we are to be found in that reconciled position.

From the time of Adam to Moses, sin had the advantage, and the stress of sin was through the Law. By Adam's offense, sin crossed over, and its end was gross death that killed so many and would kill us all to hell—if a saving gift had not arrived. Grace and Death are two opposing specters in our lives. Death, an early and unexpected force, was birthed when Adam sinned and God sighed, and death felt its vital power from the glee of condemnation, whereby it set out to change God's breath in man into a vapor. Meanwhile, the generations of man huffed along, making only small eddies in the large and windy gasp of Death. By one man death entered, but by another grace appeared. If this grace and the gift of righteousness have been given to us, how much more will we reign in life through Jesus Christ, who has eternal life.

The air is now clear, and the clouds are white. The thorn, which had never wished to be so sharp, awaits what you may bring with inspiration, awaits to have its point changed to a bloom. Isaiah the prophet says of this, that where once only mopes were possible, the wilderness and the wasteland will exhale itself ebullient. The desert will be happy and will have its dry stick turn into a rose.

A clever person may ask how this can be. While we were still unbelievers and importuned to fend off pestering and aversive life with fleshy strength, and we had only dry answers to our wet cries, God came up with a brilliant plan. The effort of sacrifice and blood was sufficient for forgiveness of sin, but the problem lay deeper: the fruit had learned its poison from the root, which had at any rate the ambition for the whole mess. And in order for the old mistake of sin to no longer repeatedly crop up in human lives, the aggravating root had to be chopped. God not only took care of sin but also of the sinful nature of the spirit of man. The way God won over this seeming impossible problem was to—in the moment of belief in Christ—co-crucify the tainted spirit of the believer to a very real death. But God does not leave you empty or the chamber of your soul virginal; He does not keep you dead.

Instead He matches you up in an instant with your royal mate, who becomes to you an uncreated breath, the spirit of Christ, whom your soul will forever breathe in.

You are a new breed, and you can face sin from your new, resurrected side. You have died and are free from sin. Meanwhile, your winning is not only because of death. Indeed, you are alive, and that only to your Father, who has birthed you with His very seed and, in a way, begotten you with His private essence. See to it, therefore, since He has given you His own life, that you keep Him not as a mere guest in the guest chamber of your roomy soul, as if through a old habit to prefer the leftover sediment of your past and murky heart. Instead let Him into your proximity with tender inhalations, because, as you will discover, His spice is carried on a gentle wind.

If you only have the least acquaintance with Him, and you think you are still the congenital offspring of your old self, then the ghost of guilt will drift again inside and bring with it familiar thoughts. But you should not mix your new mind with the strange grave of the past. Don't look back like Lot's wife to discover what once was. You can express yourself enthusiastically and righteously, because you have the emanating example inside. Do not be confused in thinking that righteousness is too narrow in its extent. It is your new life, and there is not allowed any condemnation anymore for those who are in Christ.

I suspect you are feeling constrained to oppose this too-good news, a too-good and easy salvation with too many advantages. You assume that a little guilt would be more proper, a correct ingredient added into the pure blood of the Lamb. I really do not know why you want to coexist like this. That which man could not do by works or by guilt, God did by sending His own Son in the likeness of sinful man, by whom He therefore condemned all sin. But this redemption begins inside, and if you are so anxious to make a work of it, to be a slave, then vigorously strain to live in the spirit and avoid the carnal mind to which you are so long used to.

Can it be true that you care for the knowledge of righteousness rather than the righteousness that knowledge brings? And be careful also of what may deceive you, as some have even said and accused us of: that we can now sin more and it no longer matters, because grace abounds with sin. But I think these accusers have obstinately dug in their heels, thinking themselves instructive, when they for their own sakes try to keep you from your full redemption. This freedom is too sudden for them; they are afraid they may be found unbound with no chain of slavery to bind them to their joyous sense of order. If you are happier with some sort of chain and wish for a hard passage and look toward obedience as a necessary star in the sky of sprinkled truth, then by all means live upright and clean as though you are a slave to righteousness.

Our great and true state of righteousness does not dissolve our sense of rationality into ignorance; our conscience is present to remind us of sin, that it still occurs in spite of our state. And what can we say of this? We are aware that our flesh wanders off in its own deathward walk, but it is no longer we who have a passage into the night. It is sin that dwells inside, sin that does this on its own. In the past, I found myself divided, with the flesh unsure and unwilling to come to its muddy end, while my spirit, certain and keen, was willing to take off into eternal and holy flight; but now I am learning to reckon myself outside of the ambition of the flesh. My old self, having been provoked by death, still attempts without my consent to slowly heal its wound through an unhappy process of finding worth and God. But I am refusing the symptoms or struggle of the old self, and I consider myself whole, as I actually am in Christ.

Given all of this, we should not import from this amazing grace any excuse to sin. Instead we give our obligation, our body, in holiness to God. With a heart full of new things, then, we make sure our love is real, not swollen to hypocrisy nor hidden as in anxious constraint. Your neighbor, brother, or sister may be still of clay, but love them tenderly anyway, as one who understands. A slippery animal may live in their pond, a thorny rank plant may grow where their roses ought, but you are tender toward them. You do not look for fresh trouble when you exceed them in some way. Now that you have so plenteously attained an understanding, make sure some commentary of it is kept for yourself, by which you will make sure that your opinion is not higher than yourself.

I have for many years wanted to come to visit you, and though, for the time being, the motions of my love for you is confined to letters, I will break loose and let my love have its full vent when I come to see you on my way through Spain. I ask you also, in moments when you think of me, to strive along with me in prayer, making room for me in your requests, that I will be delivered from those who do not believe as we do. For these people, the truth has fallen to the side. The grey old tree stands lonely on the plain, and on its broken branches there is only bark to tell the root which way to grow, to tell the trunk of a nearby youthful seed that has taken growth within the dust. But the tree is old and pale and in respite; it has no mood for change or life; it mocks the seed and curses its growth as a mere transient aspirant. Of the new tree, Isaiah says, there is a root of Jesse, and He will grow and reign over the Gentiles, and in Him all the peoples will find hope. By reason of this hope, I encourage you to keep yourselves firm.

Give my greeting to Priscilla and Aquila, they are fellow workers with me for the gospel. Indeed, they have risked their lives for my life. Greet also the church that meets in their house, and Mary, who went out of her way to help us.

Paul

Chapter 26

⊰ ✖ ⊱

Letter of Paul to the Corinthians:

To the church of God in Corinth, to you who in every place call on the name of Jesus Christ our Lord: greetings.

In many ways I am taken by you. Yes, it is true that I am very glad for you all, that God has give you so much grace through His Son, insomuch as you have an abundance of gifts and come short in none. On the other hand, and I was told this by some people of Chloe's house, some other thing has asserted itself with prejudice among you. By way of this, one would say, "I follow Paul," and another would say, "I'm of Peter," and yet another, "I'm of Christ." Let me really get down to it: is Christ divided? We cannot squander the unity of Christ on our private excitements, setting up new and frivolous foundations of various cliques.

Because of your divisions, I find out that you are still babies in the spirit, and by this I mean you are still carnal and need to be fed with milk. Solid food is a thing out of reach, hiding on the shelves, preserved and waiting for when you stand up on the discipline of your spiritual feet. In the expectation of your growth, many instructors have come your way; they are all persuaded to have you grow beyond the cot. Yet all this honor has seemed to confuse or agitate you into different factions. These instructors are no less than God's fellow workers for your sakes. You are

God's field. One, after the pattern of a farmer, plants seed, and another, in the same sense, waters the seed. Between these hands you should not choose or give discordant preference; it is God who gives the increase.

I may have laid the foundation, but another comes along, sees that you are born, and builds upon your life. I have, in hope, a groundwork made of gold, a foundation made of silver and of gems. There is no other foundation than this precious One, than Jesus Christ. Another teacher may come and lay down a diverting plank and make you into scaffolding, make you into hay and straw; but each worker's work will be revealed for what it is on the Day of fire, when each deed will be priced with exceeding heat.

Mankind lives between the day and night, and their minds wish for the death of the protracted dim. The day died when Adam fell, and the dusk took over our early dawn. Still, God did not leave the sun and moon to spin halfheartedly, their gaze with drooping lids. The sun has risen with healing in its wings, and its ray seeks for you as for a flower. It is a new dispensation, an age in which all things are yours—whether of Paul or Peter or Apollos. All things present and all things to come, all are yours. And you are Christ's, and Christ is God's. Though you have many instructors, I take the merit as your father, in that I was the first to bring you the gospel, and because of this I have an obligation for concern.

Now the message we are preaching is the cross of Christ. For those who will perish, this message makes no sense. Where are the apparent wise people of this world? They are proud to see past all things, glad to be an edifice of sunlight and affirmation for themselves and all the little ones beneath. Nonetheless, it is God's wisdom to bring the wisdom of the world to nothing. For the Greek, the message of the cross is not fibrous enough and cannot instantly pose upright on the bones and tendons of human philosophy, which has its point or anchor on the shores of clay. For the Jew, who reaches higher and is not afraid of heaven and the stars, comes the fanciness of a sign, which if reckoned right, will be the firm ground of their faith. Yet the foolishness of God is wiser than the wisdom of men, and the apparent weakness of God is stronger than the strength of men.

For the moment, I am sending Timothy to you that he may tell you of my way of life and how to emulate my ways in Christ. I think some of you betray a little pride, as though I am not coming to you to see for myself, but I will be coming to you shortly and will see whether those who have an imposing grandstand among you have their pose in words alone or in power, because the kingdom of God invariably shows itself in power.

Where both a rod and gentleness are possible, I would so much rather and more distinctly come with the spirit of the latter and of love. When I come, I am ready to be reduced to the one by determination—or to the other with ready sympathy and pleasure. This is because I have heard of sexual immorality among some of you, where a man has his father's wife! I suppose that even unbelievers do not do this sort of thing. When you meet up together, you should deal with this properly, as it is no less than leaven in your fellowship. What will it be when it grows throughout the lump? Do what you can while you still have a shaping hour. Though your hearts are like doves, tender and quivering, you ought to know that love sinks not in the sight of sin. It is good for love to rush against the contaminant and spit out the leavened bread. Earthly love loves to overlook, loves the superficial blur, but divine love sees something more, loves more, does not come short.

Therefore, once the lump has been purged and this man returns pure, being consonant with repentance—because that is the goal and effective point of it all—you should turn to him with the ready love that had looked after him in the first place.

I recall the letter you wrote to me and the many questions therein, among which is the inevitable question of foods offered to idols. First off, knowledge is fine, but you should be careful of yearning for it, that you may not by accident discover your minds full and your hearts void. Again, knowledge is good and useful;

let your eyes look on it, but let your lips not kiss after it. I say this because some have become up puffed-up, making room for their marvelous learning and lore. Meanwhile, do not leave love out; it will better edify.

Now, concerning whether a believer can eat food that was once offered to idols, we know nothing to impute to these gods. Really, there is only one God, the Father and our Lord Jesus Christ. You may eat without offense. You have the advantage of knowledge, a freedom from the narrow constraints of the law or the too-easy rebuke of an uncertain conscience that is full of drive but empty of truth. Notwithstanding your full view of freedom, you should consider the new or weak believer whose theology is still ruined by the past, having been raised up on the anger of God rather than His perfect love.

For the sake of their weakness, then, I will be overly careful, adding trouble on myself, and not eat such food. I know I am subtracting myself from my due freedom in this way, but I become all things to all men that in some way I may win them to God. Can I take a wife as the other apostles do? Could I expect donations from you to support my call? I can do all these, but I have in my race bridled myself like a warhorse. My reins are strict, and my feet are shod with silver shoes. I gallop straight and undeterred. I become the least, that I may get a high reward.

Concerning spiritual gifts, I have a few things to advise. When you come together to meet, one has a supernatural word, one has gifts of healing, one a prophecy, one an expression with an unknown tongue—all from the Holy Spirit as He distributes and sees fit. The gifts are not meant for waste or pomp, and each person should be mindful of the diversity, of the order of things, so that the Spirit's gentle push might not be for you an incitement of envy of another's shine or an inopportune pressing on your part to gain the gaze of eyes that were meant for Him.

We are one body made up of many members, and the body functions better when the members are not hesitating or wrangling their proper state. Will the foot, feeling inferior, say it is less because it is not the hand? Or will the ear, feeling low in a bad sense, excuse itself from the body because it is not the eye? At the same time, the eye should not in its assuming hold itself up too high. No, there is a general diffusion of honor among the members. Each part fits, and each part is needed. You may not be the lips that receive the kiss, but you may be the heart, drawn back and silent, which can give the love. Everyone ought to take his place. Some are apostles, some prophets, some teachers, some workers of miracles. Keep in mind that your heart is greater than your gift; guard that the gift stays a light and not a sword, that the way of the gift has ways in love, because that is the more excellent way.

So then, remain in humility, and let your love help you endure. You know what is best. Love and gifts are not equal; pursue the first and desire the second.

I should point out again the reason for all my exertion, which is a message that I had received and delivered to you: that Jesus Christ died for our sins, that He was buried, that He rose again on the third day, according to the prediction of the Scriptures. And then, perhaps, as though to detract from the skepticism of the unbelieving mind, He appeared to Peter and to the twelve— and also to me, as an apostle born out of time and grafted in, being no longer substituted. It is as though I want to correct this honor, feeling in myself that I should define this position with something of variance, feeling that I am the least of them all because I had persecuted the church of God. Meanwhile, I labor with something better than guilt, for I have defeated that quarrel. I have risen with the force of grace, which was not in vain, and is above the ruthless demands of condemnation and weakness, making me what I am today.

If Christ has been raised from the dead, how is it that some of you have gone on to borrow another notion that there is no resurrection of the dead? I am not sure how you can expand your hope or salvation to such a short length, because, if the dead are not raised, then Christ had not been raised, and your believing is to your own inconvenience. If the benefit of the cross approaches only to our natural life on earth, then it may be better to say, "Let us eat and drink uninhibited, because tomorrow we die anyway!" You should know that by the cross all things have been made subject to Him—even death.

Someone has taken notice of a degraded body, and in view of that, his or her faith refuses to go as far as God's power, insomuch as this person ponders the raised body through disturbing pictures. Though the natural body goes to sleep, it does like a seed dissolve underground, and again, like a seed, it drinks from the celestial soil and grows up into another form. The body is sown to spend itself upon sepulchral earth, but it feels itself no slave. It scorns whatever withered marks are marking it for death. It waits upon the cross and God, whose spirit wind flutters over the hard sod and whose whisper wakes the shout of your eternal exultation.

Of the many things that you give off—little breezes of the Eternal Wind—make sure that some approach a gale. I mean by this that the odor of Christ can be smelled, a fragrance which is taken from the garden of good deeds, specifically your generosity. In light of this, I recommend you take up collections on the first day of the week. Perhaps by this method you can take something from time, because time might be for you too firm when you want to give of your prosperity at once.

Now I am coming to you when I travel through Macedonia; I may even stay the winter with you. At that time I will pick up the collection, and we can send it off as a gift to Jerusalem. If Timothy comes to visit you, see that he is treated with respect. His youth may be taken for easy bait by the mind that trades still through the flesh, but work yourself out of this perceived advantage. Let Timothy do the work of the Lord without fear. The Christians of Asia send their greetings, as do Aquilla and Priscilla and the people who meet in their house. My love is with all of you, amen.

Chapter 27

— ⋖ ✖ ⋗ —

Letter of Paul to the Galatians:

To the churches in Galatia, grace and peace to you from God the Father and our Lord Jesus Christ. I am surprised that you who had once loved the gospel now love something else, that you had taken hold of the proper root but now wait for the fruit of your own mutable trunk, that you are turning away from grace to another gospel.

I know there are teachers who have come in with other doctrines, strange sprigs and encumbering branches that by their bulk and shadows are meant to overbuild the simplicity of the gospel into a perversion. The gospel that I have preached to you was not received by me through man. I received it from Jesus Christ Himself.

You all know my past, how my eyes were completely and only open to Judaism, and this fixed and factious sight set me at odds with the church of God and sustained my destruction of His people. I was enlivened with the thunder and storm that zeal can bring, a mean storm that willed me not to look at sensibility. I progressed beyond my contemporaries in the study of the Law, in Judaism, and I think I progressed even beyond myself. I think I took my zeal for truth; it had sundered me, and I had planned to sunder life. In my own mind, I was quite content to be the steersman of tradition, of my own and ardent course through the sea of life, but God had called me while I was in another water, in my mother's womb, and was pleased to revealed His Son in me. Since then I have been preaching the gospel, and the dictates of labor and tradition have dissolved into the precepts of freedom.

Soon after I was converted, I went to Arabia, and after about three years, I returned to Jerusalem in order to meet Peter, with whom I then stayed for about two weeks. Subsequently, and for fourteen years, I remained in the regions of Syria and Cilicia, at which point I returned again to Jerusalem. This time around, I went to check with the leaders whether the gospel I had been preaching was compatible with their message. I communicated my gospel to them in private, almost as an unsure man in a corner, to see whether I was outside the current of truth. At that time some brothers—false brothers, I may add—came in and took some of my message for partiality, for error. But the substance of their criticism was an invention, and I and the brothers who came with me were not enfeebled by their words or their standing.

We withstood them and kept our stance, unwilling to have our freedom in Christ, bought by His blood, reduced to the bondage of some clever fellow's tradition or private abstraction. Their fine speaking and declamatory expression could not persuade me to flex or alter my gospel, and Titus, who was with me at the time and did not have any enthusiasm for the demands of their mixed doctrines, refused to be circumcised. My exertion paid off, and in time, James, Peter, and John gave us the right hand of fellowship, recognizing my gospel on equal terms, though believing that mine is better suited for the Gentiles. Theirs would be appropriated to the Jewish Christians, who by tradition and ostentation—and a little pedantry—prefer to add the merit of circumcision to the salvation brought by the blood of Christ.

We left it at that. I had made my point. I am convinced of the blood of Christ, believing that no other import of blood—in this case by circumcision—nor other compensation—whether a

rusty tradition or an enthusiastic craze—can add to the freedom
we have in Christ. I will tell you about another incident that
happened when I was in Antioch and about how fast the worm
comes out in spring, however ready it is, hungry for the death
our leaves. I am speaking figuratively of our salvation and the
tree of life of which we eat. It is simply true that for some people
the night is lovelier than the day, and they sleeplessly work to
force their shade onto our light. Be careful, then, of the length
of your light, because their shade is meant for dusk. Even our
beloved Peter was caught confused when the twilight took him
by surprise.

Both Peter and I were in Antioch at the time, and we were
having a meal with the non-Jewish people, that is, the Gentiles.
While we were eating together, Jewish Christians from Jerusalem,
sent by James, came over to visit us. Suddenly I saw Peter show
symptoms of hesitancy; he tried to correct a situation that was
an object of scrutiny to the brothers from Jerusalem, as these
brothers would sneer at a commingling of Jews and Gentiles,
making an unequal distinction between them. Even Barnabas,
who has worked with me, was caught up in this impulse, and for
a moment his insight meant less to him than the approving eye
of the visitors.

When I saw Peter disguising himself by his withdrawal from
us, I spoke up, being unable to keep quiet through the scene that
was silently playing out. I said to Peter, in front of everyone, that
he was wrong. How could we force the Gentiles to live in the
Jewish traditions? Our justification before God is not made up of
hard labor through obedience to the Law or tradition, nor does
our justification lie somewhere in between sweat and blood. It is
by faith in His blood that we are justified. So then, we are wrong
when we try to rebuild what He has taken away. You are born
too late; the age of grace is here. I am sure those in graves, who
were once under the Law, would frown, if they could, on your
desire to walk back miles into the past—to what has sunk into the
earth, to history that shows the tombs of man, to man's separation

from God, to disqualified hearts, to discouraged minds, to arms too weak.

It is not that the Law is pointless; it was actuated to clarify sin and was borrowed for my death, by which I was co-crucified in all its penalties with Christ. The advantage of the cross is not my death but my resurrection into life. Indeed, I live a sort of substituted life, where a native spirit has evolved me instantly into another self—the being of Christ Himself, who lives in me with the force of an inseparable fusion.

It makes me wonder, oh naive Galatians, why you are leaning back, why you have let the flame of the new spirit burn out, why you have loosened and relaxed your hold, only to go back to the empty monuments of your past to try your luck with them. It baffles me that you wish again to shuffle around in the musty rituals that do not give life. Perhaps you go back to these old things because they are familiar to your late fear, or perhaps you still, in ignorance, feel you may charm God by your good life. Perhaps you say to yourself, "Yes, I will make a little law for myself unto God. I will break into His heart by my maneuver, and I will be broad enough with good behavior and intent to pass the standard of His holiness."

Really, your thinking is foolish. I do not know how else to say it. It was faith that got you saved, not strength. How is it that you now want to give strength an equal place? There is only one Spirit who gives salvation, yet there is another left on earth that can cause a curse. It is written that anyone who is under the Law is under a curse, because the Law is the curse for anyone who cannot perfectly obey its demands. Do you understand my surprise, then, when I heard that you who once had burst out into life and freedom through faith were now shrinking to meet God halfway, as it were? Your hearts may be great, yet your minds are not. Your thoughts want you to make your harvest in between two fields. What kind of fruit can grow from confused seed, from a planting in between the spirit and the Law? Are you making your own brand of salvation?

Remember, when a contract or covenant is made, a certainty is brought to it, and it is admitted by every party that no alterations can be made. Even so, an agreement—in this case, the Law of Moses—cannot casually look forward without looking to the past and cannot override a promise made four hundred and thirty years prior to its establishment. Back then, a promise was made to Abraham and his Seed—that is, Christ. It was an agreement unconquered by the private maneuvers of men, the intrusions of the Devil, or the enthusiasm of the Law. It is not that the Law has error or is in error; the promise of blessing to Abraham and to Christ makes inevitable and perfect use of the Law to fulfill itself. How does it do that? What is the point of the Law, anyway? The Law of Moses reaches out to the fuzzy elements of morality and sin, to the muddiness of half-good goodness, to the rationality of justice, to intolerant holiness, to impatient death, to the demands of our nemesis, to the weakness of mankind—and coolly encapsulates them all. And for a moment when it does so, we seem to be at such a loss over the squadrons that are about us and the guards that help us no more than death. But then, thank God, someone was better than the Law and had a glad triumph over it, and He now shares His outstanding victory with us through our faith.

A teacher teaches, we assume, with pleasure at the prospect of the student's advancement. The Law also tries out its long, instructive powers in hope and in spite of itself to bring us to Christ. But now the Law has concluded itself. Rather, it is concluded by Christ and is convinced that we, who are in Christ, are admitted to rank of the grown, to the place of the perfect. Before Jesus Christ came and fulfilled the Law, we had the misfortunes of a slave, the trouble with fear, and the weariness of failure, because a slave fails from the start, and the master's face does not change to help. However, once we believe in Christ and the work of the cross, we are automatically born again, as it were, into sonship, and we are all sons of God. There are no longer slaves, no longer Jew or Greek, male or female. We are actually one with Christ's spirit; we are all one. And if we are born as sons, our hearts and lips cry out properly, "Daddy, Daddy!" We are born of God and are His heirs. This is the good news of the gospel, and I am sure that at one time you understood this message and had set it up in this way for your happiness and peace. Why is it, then, that you look again to things that will put you into bondage, into slavery?

I hear you have begun again to observe rituals, that you observe certain days and seasons as if these assist in your salvation. Honestly, I am afraid for you. It seems to me that you no longer understand what Christ has done. Prior to Christ, your efforts were consumed by the Law. It insensibly defeated all your struggles to stand perfectly before God, and yet you are not exhausted by this; you are ready again to give up liberty. You noiselessly tie the chains around yourself, yet these chains, your former guards, are loud witnesses of things more free than what once was.

They tell of Abraham, and they tell their figurative forecast of the two sons of Abraham—one from a free woman and the other from a bondwoman. It was Abraham who laid aside for a moment the promise of God and aspired, with the impatient subtleties of the flesh, to fulfill God's word by means of the flesh. And he was with Hagar, the slave, who conceived a son. But the son born through the flesh did not have his triumph, nor did his mother. Both contracted the strictness of the Scripture that called for the casting out of Ishmael, because he was not to share in the inheritance of the son of the freewoman, who would be Isaac. This figure uses Ishmael to represent the current Hebrew who is under the bondage of the flesh and the personal effort to obtain worth, the Hebrew who looks to the pregnant Law of Moses, his mother, for his impossible birth to salvation.

We who believe in Christ are of Isaac, of the spirit, of the promise, of the stars of heaven. Our distant brothers of the earth and the sands moan against us with an uncertain edge and aim their first-thought feeling up at us to bring us down to them. It is now as it was then and as it always will be: the one born of the flesh persecutes the one born of the spirit. Now we are of the spirit, and our righteousness, our salvation, is by faith. Since we are born of the spirit, what is sown in us should come up as fruit. The earthly, fleshy nature of our past selves is dead; it has been crucified with Christ.

Therefore, let your memory begin with Christ. Let it not dream again of the tendencies of the old nature or seek the voice of the echo that speaks according to your familiar past of adultery, coarseness, hatred, envy, murder, drunkenness, and so on. You have been interrupted by death, by resurrection, by the growth of a new tree who is Christ, and from now on your common fruit should be His, which is without shame and not false. When you reach for them, they are no longer truant. Your fruits are better and truly born, and among these are love, joy, peace, patience, kindness, goodness, self-control, and strength.

Perhaps you are like a fledgling, moving about as a tenderfoot in your new capacity. But be certain about that which is subsiding and that which is true of your new heart—a sort of lion-heart, which has enough beat to carry you focused throughout this life. You are of the spirit; you are the white rose in a strange soil; you keep your color and your peace, even when the brown soil or some other common planting laughs at you because you seem so odd, so imported and far-off derived.

Yet even for those who are born-again, the tremor of the old flesh makes itself felt. It stirs and makes us turn as though we hear the voice of the old tyrant, who, though dead, acts to our fears as if we are yet destined to be condemned. If someone does sin, and sin has the advantage, then one of you who is temperate and mature should go and help this person. Meanwhile, be careful, you who are the counselor, that you yourself are not tempted with sin, because when we correct someone else, presumption immediately volunteers its labor to us, and with it the spirit of pride. Though your righteousness lies now quite outside of sin—or rather exists in spite of sin—you should regard the natural laws of life, under which there are things like sowing and reaping; and for sure, if you constantly conceive fleshy or carnal spurs, you will reap something of them in this life. In respect to the same, it is better to sow according the spirit so that you can reap everlasting life.

Remain in life, then, because death is not dead, but eternal life has victory over death. In this natural life, death does come all year long, not overtly but with soft tendrils. Yet death itself has begun to doubt you, because you are a new creation, and your buds and blooms have their long life at the foot of resurrected life.

Remind yourselves that you are new, and keep to this basic rule. In this way you will have peace and relieve me of trouble, because I have had enough of it. Let the grace of our Lord Jesus be with your spirit, amen.